CYPRUS

CYPRUS

Photography Gerhard P. Müller
Text Klaus Liebe

Readers: Petra Altmann, Dieter Löbbert
Graphic Layout: Christine Hartl, Bertram Schmidt
Production: Johannes Eikel
English Translation: Carolyn Lawson

Title page: Playing cards

© 1984, 1986 (for the English edition)
by Verlag C.J. Bucher GmbH,
Munich and Lucerne

Contents

An Island between East and West

Nikos Kazantzakis, the great Greek author, saw in Cyprus the twin-sister to his own homeland Crete – the two islands, however, not being identical twins: Crete, manly and unfriendly, full of pride and heroic rigour, overwhelming, a danger to any conqueror; Cyprus, open and receptive, alluring and mysterious, a tiny patch of earth to whose charm one cannot help but succumb, the charm of the eastern Levant. "I never saw an island," he recorded, "that had such a feminine character, I never breathed air so full of sweet, dangerous temptation."

Since mythological times, when the Goddess of Love, Aphrodite, born out of the foam of the waves, stepped onto land here, this allure has held all newcomers spellbound. But the history of Cyprus has shown another side of this picture: an island of tears and blood that has been paying for its geographical position since time immemorial.

The island was and is of great strategic importance. It lies at the centre of what was the most important area for the historical and cultural development of mankind: Egypt, Mesopotamia, Anatolia, Greece. The rise and fall of these civilisations have coloured and shaped Cyprus. With the changing power structures in the region the island has been subjected to many experiences, not always pleasant, by which it has been both formed and suppressed. Its fate always lay in the hands of other powers, its position was too attractive to allow it to be overlooked. Cyprus has never really discovered itself throughout its long history and that it could never be any different was made clear in this pithy statement by Benjamin Disraeli, who was Prime Minister when Great Britain took over the administration of Cyprus from the Ottoman Empire in 1878: "Cyprus is the key to Western Asia."

In order to reign supreme in the Eastern Mediterranean a hundred years ago, it was important for Great Britain as a colonial power to control Cyprus. From Cyprus it was possible to secure and control the sea and commercial routes to Britain's most important colony, India. With the opening of the Suez Canal in 1869 the strategic importance of Cyprus became even greater, and so Great Britain secured control of this Mediterranean island immediately before the Berlin Congress in 1878 at which the European powers met to divide the assets of the disintegrating Ottoman Empire. Then in a countermove the British later supported the Sultan at the Congress itself while Bismarck, acting as "honest broker", nevertheless tried to protect German interests in Turkey. Again the British were interested in protecting the overland route to India which led through Anatolia and Arabia, both of which had remained Turkish.

If we skip a hundred years and take a quick look at a map of the world today, it is easy to see that Disraeli's brief analysis is more apt and relevant than ever before. Cyprus is today, for the power which controls it, even more important than it was then. One can see that the island, which has an area of 9261 sq.km. and is the third largest in the Mediterranean after Sicily and Sardinia, is like an unsinkable aircraft carrier anchored in the Near East war zone.

The British knew exactly why they wanted to secure two sovereign military bases here when they gave Cyprus independence in 1960. It may sound paradoxical, but the position of the island right in the middle of an area of mini-crises is ideal. So it is not surprising that the island itself has so often since 1955 dominated the headlines with its own longstanding conflicts. The Israeli-Arab conflict, the Palestinian question, the rivalry between Syria and Egypt, the bloody struggle for power in the Lebanon, the seemingly unending friction between Greece and

Turkey, which to some extent is over Cyprus – all of these are being played out near at hand. So it is possible from Cyprus, due to its strategic location, to exercise influence in the area in general, a political and military presence is thus secured. Disraeli's remark would today probably be formulated as follows: from Cyprus it is possible, within a flight-time of less than one hour, to secure the oilfields in the Gulf which are so important to the West and Japan.

At the centre of foreign power interests

This is and was and, one fears, appears likely to remain Cyprus' fate. For thousands of years great power interests have collided here. There were always new conquerors who made for the island, established themselves and then were expelled. Any power from the East, from the early civilisations of the Tigris and Euphrates or the Nile, which tried to expand to the West made for Europe through Cyprus: the legendary fighting people of the Hyksos, the Egyptians, Phoenicians, Assyrians and Persians, one often taking over control from the other more than once, followed by the Ptolemies of Egypt, later the Arabs and to some extent even the Ottoman Turks who ruled Cyprus from 1571 to 1878.

And the thrust from the West was no different: the Achaean Greeks, Alexander the Great, the Roman and Byzantine Empires, the English King Richard the Lionheart, the Knights Templar and the Crusaders, the French House of Lusignan, the city states of Genoa and Venice and finally Great Britain; and today the immediate confrontation between the Greek-Byzantine Christian and the Turkish-Islamic-Oriental cultures in Cyprus itself. In view of the abundance and colourfulness of this scenario, one needs little imagination to see how history and destiny have become one for the island. The currents which have passed over Cyprus are so many and so deep that it is hardly possible to list them all or to evaluate them.

So it is even more surprising, in fact it seems almost miraculous, that the people themselves are not a mixture of all the peoples and cultures which have for thousands of years held sway over the island, but that life in Cyprus to a large extent has remained homogeneous. Around the

7

middle of the second millenium B.C., that is at about the turning-point of the middle to late Bronze Age, the first thrust of Achaean settlers reached Cyprus from the Greek mainland about 1000 km. away. Later, according to legend, many of the Greek heroes of the Trojan War were left behind in Cyprus after the victory, so that around 1180 B.C. Greek city states were founded, the island colonised and since then Cyprus has had its Greek character. This is true even today: around eighty per cent of the population consider themselves Greek. Their language and religion confirm this and they feel themselves to be an integral part of the Greek nation. So for them Cyprus is a Greek island, whose Hellenic identity is unquestionably established just as the character, life and culture of this Mediterranean island has been for more than three thousand years.

This is disputed by their Turkish compatriots. They make up about twenty percent of the population, but for them Cyprus is in no way exclusively stamped by its Greekness, exactly the opposite. They point to the importance of the three hundred years of Turkish rule in the annals of Cyprus' history. They point to the lasting and deep influence of Islam side by side with the autocephalous Greek Orthodox Church and the fact that they as Turks have put down roots here. They do not see themselves as a minority, as they are so arrogantly dismissed in the elitist thinking of the Greek Orthodox Church. The Turkish Cypriots see themselves as a community with equal rights to the island. They want to live with the Greeks with full equal rights in Cyprus.

These two very different points of view are the core of the highly explosive Cyprus problem today. There are other contributing factors, both internal and external, but in the end the tragedy of Cyprus is that, although the island is culturally a Greek island with a Greek majority, it has never belonged to the Greek state. The age-long desire of the Greek Cypriots for union with the Greek mainland, for "Enosis", is understandable and can be explained in terms of the natural development of Cyprus. In fact this idea has provided the fuel which has led the island to become the powder-keg of the Eastern Mediterranean, since for the Turkish Cypriots there is no question of allowing the island, which is also their homeland, to unite with Greece. Cyprus has a population of about 680,000, of which 510,000 are of Greek and 125,000 of Turkish origin. The rest is made up of a few thousand Armenians and Maronites, as well as about 30,000 to 40,000 Turks from the Anatolian mainland, who were moved from their homeland and resettled in Cyprus after the partition of the island in 1974. In the eyes of Greek Cypriots, these new settlers are not considered Turkish Cypriots but Turks from the mainland, a very important difference. Since the last census in 1960 no exact figures are available from either the Greek or the Turkish side, so one has therefore to work from the proportions which were established then: 77.1 per cent Greeks, 18.2 per cent Turks, 4.7 per cent others (Armenians, Maronites, British). The proportion of each community to the total population has always played a leading role in the discussion of the Cyprus problem.

Bound by tradition

At this point let us leave politics for a moment and take a trip through Cyprus, this unique treasure-trove of art and varied landscapes. Cyprus, although it is so ancient, impresses the visitor as a young, lively world. It lives out of its myths and legends which provide a counter-point to the new and practical. It is an island of surprises and even old Cyprus hands who have known the island and its people for years always find something new and unexpected. One may have travelled every mile and every path in Cyprus and then still discover something new. One remains a stranger. But a stranger is as heartily welcomed by Cypriots, Greeks and Turks alike, as one of their own: "kopiaste", please stay, join us, make yourselves at home. Hospitality is the oldest and most attractive characteristic of the Cypriots. Another is their curiosity. There is hardly another folk that is so interested in what others do and do not do – who is doing business with whom, why a certain young lady is not yet married, what the neighbours' financial state is like. Nothing remains secret for long and most things come to light before the day dawns. This is

Cyprus offers fascinating landscapes. Hang-gliding near Kourion.

the typical island mentality: whatever comes from the outside is of interest since one knows in any case what is going on in the island and things to talk and gossip about are limited.

One should also mention another characteristic of the Cypriots: their basic honesty. The number of times people go away on a trip without even locking the front door would make a European detective's hair stand on end. Burglary and theft are almost unknown and on the rare occasions when they do occur, are the subject of strong social proscription. Cars are never locked as a matter of course, and keys and documents are left inside. When the waiter or postmistress gives you change you can put it in your pocket without even counting it. If it ever happens that it does not come out right, then it is purely and simply a mistake. This happens more often that it otherwise would, since most Cypriots still think in terms of the old currency of colonial times which is long since a thing of the past. Shillings and piastres have both been discarded and the division of the pound into a thousand mils has been replaced by the more universally acceptable division into one hundred cents. Nevertheless, in spite of all the confusion, it still comes out right in the end. To be honest and upright is the most important commandment and Cypriots are still surprisingly uninfluenced by all the less pleasant levantine customs or the excesses which rapidly expanding tourism seems inevitably to bring with it.

The visitor feels sheltered in this human atmosphere and the real warmth that comes from the people of Cyprus is perhaps the most important experience the visitor will carry away with him. The more you move away from the coast, where the concrete jungle of mass tourism is spreading like a cancer, and move into the interior of the island, the more you will come upon a country and people for whom time has in no way stood still (in the sense of the cliché) but for whom the old world and its morals and values still have a meaning today. One should not be misled by the colourful bustle of the towns and seaside resorts. The Cypriots are basically conservative and where they accept new ideas they slip into a modern skin. But their heart really lies with the tried and true. Of course, even tradition-bound Cypriot society has experienced radical change in view of the political troubles which have shaken the island from the ground up

A house in the
English colonial
style in Gladstone
Street in the Greek
sector of Nicosia
(left).

The "Four Lanterns
Hotel" in Larnaca,
a building in the
English colonial style.

in the last three decades and in view of the stormy social and economic changes in the world
which Cyprus has not escaped. It would be an illusion to think that one could keep this
Mediterranean island outside the vortex of our times, to maintain a healthy microcosm as it
were. Nevertheless every change is tested here against tradition and it is above all the strenght of
the social and religious norms which guarantees this. For the Greek Cypriots it is the influence
of their somewhat backward-looking church which colours even today many of the minor
aspects of daily life.

For the Turkish Cypriots, on the other hand, the principles and commandments of Islam
forbid the all-too-blind acceptance of new ideas. Both together make up the insular mentality:
one does not give up so easily what one has, because what one can acquire from across the sea
is in no way certain to be an improvement.

The deep attachment all Cypriots feel for their homeland can, however, be as easily
explained by a quite natural phenomenon: this island, this country encapsulated by the sea, is
a mosaic of landscapes harmoniously woven together. Cyprus can thank this interplay of
contrasting elements for her name not only as the island of love but also the island of beauty.
"From the time of our birth there is something of this in us and no power in the world can wipe
out the image of our beautiful homeland. Only at death do we give it back to the earth." This is
how it was explained to me once by an old man in a Troodos coffee shop, who had grown rich in
America and returned home to die.

The Cypriots' love of country is without precedent, it provides the reason for life and
existence for a people who are still to a large extent influenced by rural ways, who see their town
merely as a village grown large. "My village" – the visitor will hear this in every conversation and
it is more than a description of place, it is a whole philosophy: the village, the house, the garden,
the flowers and the fields are the world out of which I am made, to which I belong. For people in
a highly mobile Western industrialised society it is difficult to understand this fully, but once
one has understood that a Cypriot's identity is made up of the microcosm of his village then one

begins to get a feeling for the mental suffering into which hundreds of thousands of people were plunged due to the war in 1974.

Almost 200,000 people, about 40 per cent of the population, fled to the south from the north of the island at the time of the Turkish invasion, leaving behind their villages and homes. Those who could not flee were later expelled. Conversely, thousands of Turkish Cypriots who lost their homes and land in the south of the island were resettled in the north. As a result of the Turkish invasion more than a third of the population became homeless, and lost not only house and home but had to leave a piece of themselves behind: a wound which, for both Greeks and Turks, will continue to fester for many years.

The Greek-Turkish conflict

Anyone who speaks indifferently of the north and south of Cyprus and believes the fact that one area is Greek and the other Turkish solves the problem after so many years of unrest, since it at least establishes clear boundaries and clear relationships on the island, is in fact unthinkingly ignoring the realities of the situation. It is true that since 1974/5, since the partition of their joint homeland, Greek and Turkish Cypriots have lived as two totally separate communities. It is also true that this unnatural partition has put a provisional end to the disastrous policies for which politicians on both sides are responsible. These policies are however also the result of outside influences. Greece, Turkey, Great Britain, the United States and the Soviet Union have always been involved, sometimes more and sometimes less openly. Cyprus was and is just too important to allow the Cypriots to handle it themselves – this has always been the formula for the drama of Cyprus. The present geographic and political partition has complex causes. It looks at first glance logical, after all that has happened here, but it is fundamentally unnatural and does not correspond to the structure of Cyprus which has been formed and moulded through centuries of historical development.

Wherever one looks today one confirms with a feeling of sadness that Greeks and Turks lived together in a symbiosis unique in the otherwise tense relationship between these two nations. There never was a purely Greek or purely Turkish area. The villages were colourfully inter-spersed – here a Greek one, over the next hill a Turkish one, and a few miles further on a mixed one.

Very often the church and mosque were only a stone's throw away from each other, as for example in Peristerona, west of Nicosia, and in many other places both in the north and south. The houses and gardens of Greek families often bordered on those of their Turkish neighbours, and often the Greek and Turkish coffee-shops were opposite each other in the middle of the village. Religion and language were separate but the hard everyday life on this hot island, poor in water resources, was faced together by Greeks and Turks, as Cypriots. Anyone who wants to get a taste of this mixture, albeit a bitter aftertaste, in the face of the present partition which means that no Greek may go into the north and no Turk is allowed to leave the north to go to the south, should take a look at an old map from the end of British colonial times in 1960. Blue spots represent the Greek, red the Turkish, black the mixed villages, and olive green the few Maronite villages, and show that politicians and churchmen lie when they say that the whole island or some specific part of it has always belonged to one or the other side. Wherever one looks – be it from Cape Andreas, the monastery of the Apostle on the Carpass peninsula, the most north-easterly point of Cyprus, along the limestone mountains of the Kyrenia range as far as Cape Khormakiti in the west; or be it from Cape Akamas in the west over those fragrant fields filled with legends of love to Paphos and then on to the Akrotiri peninsula with its twin capes Zevgari and Gata, all along the south coast to Larnaca bay and to Ayia Napa, the new tourist mecca on the island, as far as Cape Greco to the south of Famagusta and then on again in an arc up to the Carpass peninsula; or be it in the interior of Cyprus, the volcanic Troodos mountain range, with its gently sinking slopes or on the hot dusty Mesaoria plain, reminiscent of the steppes in summer – wherever one looks one finds the two communities side by side and

12

Continued on page 29

Petra tou Romiou on the south-west coast of Cyprus. This is where, according to legend, Aphrodite rose out of the foam of the waves.

Overleaf: rocky coast-line on the south-west tip of Cyprus between Cape Greco and Ayia Napa.

13

The Mesaoria plain lying between the mountain peaks of Pentadaktylos in the north and Troodos in the south.

Landscape on the western foothills of the Troodos mountains.

A shepherd on the coast north of Paphos.

The sunny southern foothills of the Troodos mountains are ideal for the cultivation of vines.

Overleaf: refreshment at the well. Near Dhali.

The Church of St. Lazarus in Larnaca was built in the 9th century over the ostensible tomb of Lazarus who, according to legend, was Bishop of Larnaca. The bell-tower was added later.

Previous page: the theatre of Kourion took on its present size, with a seating capacity of about 3,500, in the 2nd century A.D.

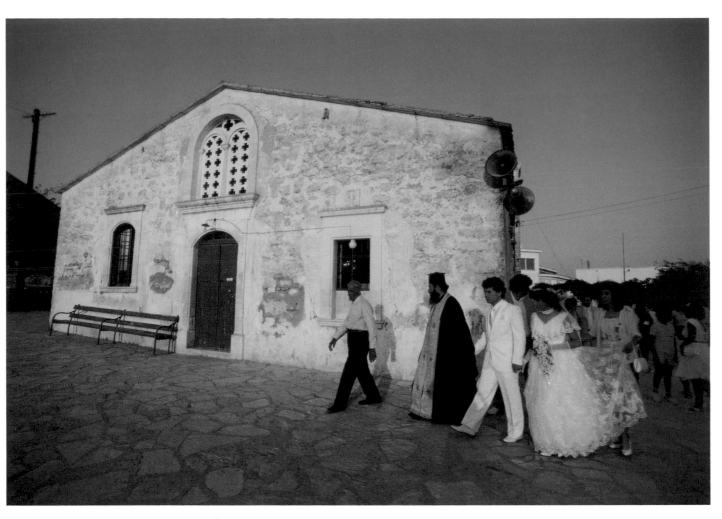

A wedding party in front of Ayia Paraskevi Church in Yeroskipos.

During the marriage ceremony.

23

The house of the village priest in Phasoula.

An evening stroll in Kato Lefkara.

Overleaf: market day in Larnaca.

28

interlaced. This has been the face of Cyprus and the world and life of her people for the last four hundred years, since the conquest of the island by the Ottoman Turks in 1570/71.

The Greeks have been forced out of the northern part of the island and the Turks have disappeared from the south. The dividing line drawn by the Turkish army in 1974, the so-called "Attila Line", cannot be crossed by either side. It begins at the western end of the Morphou bay, runs south of Lefka and Morphou through Nicosia, dividing the capital with barbed wire fences and barricades in a way reminiscent of Berlin, and sweeps in a bulge towards Famagusta where it ends again at the sea, taking in the old town which was always Turkish and the new Greek city of seaside hotels. About thirty eight per cent of the territory of the Republic of Cyprus, independent since 1960, is today occupied by Turkish troops. Twenty per cent of the population, clearly the smaller group, now controls almost double the amount of land which would be apportioned to them even on a purely mathematical basis.

In November 1983 the Turkish-controlled north declared itself an independent state and thus consolidated politically the already completed *de facto* partition of the two communities. The north is of course only recognised by Turkey which controls it with its troops. The constitutional government of Cyprus is located in the Greek area of Nicosia although its standing has been challenged by the Turkish Cypriots and Turkey since 1964.

Why does the common world of the Greek and Turkish Cypriots, which the thirty year old maps attest to, no longer function? Why did this world, which had held together for so many centuries, disintegrate in just a few years under pressure from both sides? How did the Cyprus conflict, which today seems more insoluble than ever, arise? What is the future of the island of Aphrodite in the face of so much bitterness on both sides?

At this point we must outline the history of the estrangement between Greek and Turkish Cypriots. It is an estrangement arising out of a conflict which, despite its local roots, has always had international implications and which forebodes darkly for the future. A conflict which it is not possible to solve with reason and logic – that has been tried by the United Nations and by politicians of various hues for more than a generation. It is a conflict which to Europeans seems laughable and which could easily be solved by the application of the principles of self-determination and justice.

However in Cyprus other rules apply. Here is a world in which it is not possible to come to terms with the present-day realities due to the legacy of the conflicts of the 19th century. Emotions and old anxieties, such as the Greeks' fear of the Turks and equally the long-standing arrogance of the Greeks towards the Turks, still dominate the scene. Neither side can take a calm, objective look at the problem, each side sees itself as being in the right. The mistakes, the offences, always lie on the other side. So the chronicler or observer always finds himself in the wrong when he carefully tries to find justice in the arguments of both sides.

Even the question as to when the conflict began is not a simple question of an historical date but an emotionally charged issue. Which date should one choose? 1570/71 – which marked the conquest of the island by Sultan Selim II and the terrible carnage which followed the fall of the walled cities of Nicosia and Famagusta, as well as the shameless breach of promise of the commander-in-chief Lala Mustapha to the heroic defender of the city, Marc Antonio Bragadino.

1821 – the massacre of the Greek elite, archbishop, bishops and nobility, by the Turkish Governor Kütchük Mehmed in answer to the outbreak of the Greek War of Independence on the mainland which in fact, until that fateful 9th July, had not affected this island so far away from the mainland.

1878 – the takeover of control of the island by Great Britain, an event that both communities registered with mixed feelings, since for the Turks it meant a change of status from rulers to ruled, and for the Greeks it raised the question of whether their growing desire for "Enosis" would be suppressed.

1955 – the beginning of the bitterly fought guerrilla struggle of the Greek Cypriot underground organisation EOKA (the National Organisation of Cypriot Fighters) against the British rule, for the union of Cyprus with Greece, and against the vital interests of the Turkish Cypriots.

1960 – the date when Cyprus was granted an unstable independence with a constitution which gave the Turks more rights than their numbers warranted and which the majority of Greek Cypriots therefore never accepted and tried to sabotage.

The end of 1963 and 1964, when communal strife broke out after Archbishop Makarios told his Turkish Vice-President Fazil Kütchük that he wanted to amend the constitution which he had signed four years earlier, to the detriment of the Turks. Communal strife during which the Turkish Cypriots, the substantially smaller and weaker of the two communities, paid the higher price in blood. Strife during which bands of irregulars, disappointed supporters of union with Greece, again tried to unite the whole of Cyprus with the Greek mainland through the murder and expulsion of Turkish Cypriots.

1974 – the coup against President Makarios by pro-Enosis elements and the Greek military regime, which made Nicos Sampson, self-styled "Turk Killer", president for a critical week, which in turn gave Turkey the excuse to take over the north of Cyprus in a two-phase invasion and in practice to divide the island, thus from Turkey's point of view putting an end to the conflict which had been going in for so long at the cost of thousands of dead and hundreds of thousands of refugees.

The later dates may seem the more important but the earlier ones have also had a role to play in the creation of this tragedy, because the material for this conflict comes in no way entirely from external factors, from the interests of third parties. The conflict between the two communities in Cyprus has its own special characteristics which lie in the difference in mentality of the two communal groups. It is more a socio-economic, cultural conflict coloured by religion, a failure to really communicate and to free oneself from old thought and behaviour patterns, than a simple struggle for power.

The predominantly Greek character of Cyprus which has existed for more than 3,000 years and the Greek identity of the majority of Cypriots is without question. Irrespective of who ruled the island, the Greek element always survived and absorbed foreign influence. Even though the

*Turkish notables put
their problems to the
British Governor.
Around 1880.*

island has throughout its unsettled history never belonged to the Greek state, its Greco-Byzantine character and concept of self are at least as strong and alive as that of the people on the Greek mainland. The desire, the natural longing as Archbishop Makarios called it, to eventually unite the island with Greece can therefore be explained since it coincides with the desire for self-determination. In a democratic nation the majority principle rules: the majority decides and the rights of the minority are protected. But this model, which was so cleverly written into the so-called Zurich and London Agreements to establish the constitution for the independent Republic of Cyprus, did not work for Cyprus. The reasons are many and varied and it is only possible to outline the main points which led in a few years to the shattering of the experiment and the collapse of the young independent Republic.

First of all the numerically smaller Turkish community has never thought of itself as a minority in relation to the Greek community. The Turks see themselves as an independent community with equal rights and duties. And they therefore demand equal representation in all state institutions. Their goal is a fifty-fifty arrangement although the distribution of the communities is eighty per cent Greek to twenty per cent Turkish. If the Turkish side achieves this goal then it would mean that the much smaller group was forcing its political will on the much larger one. Such a model would not function even in states which have a truly democratic tradition and much longer experience of inter-communal life. On the other hand, the Turks' view of themselves as an independent community has something to be said for it. They were for three hundred years, at the time of the Ottoman Empire, rulers of Cyprus and during British colonial rule the Turks and Greeks were never seen or treated as a minority and majority but both in the same way as inhabitants of the island, as Cypriots. The colonial rulers left religious and cultural matters to the two communities and provided the basic pre-requisites for this. In all other areas however – legal, administrative or economic – no differences were made between Greeks and Turks, at least on paper. Nevertheless the two communities, and especially the Greeks, felt easily slighted.

A shady spot to read the daily paper. In Phasoula, near Limassol.

Playing tavli, the most popular diversion for men in Cyprus (left).

A typical pastime for women: embroidery. In a village near Kyrenia.

A tradesman in Paphos (left).

A visit to the barber in Yeroskipos.

Of course the numerical inequality made itself felt in other ways. Another factor which is indispensable to the understanding of the present day conflict was the introduction in colonial times of a large number of Turkish Cypriots into the civil service. Greek Cypriots happily state this fact when they want to make the point that the British always favoured the Turks and gave them too much importance. However, it is not as simple as that, because the British merely carried on with the system they found when they took over the control of Cyprus from the Ottomans. It was a structure which had developed out of the natural proclivities and strengths of the two communities. In Cyprus the same administrative procedures were followed as elsewhere in the Ottoman Empire, the only ones that were feasible for this enormous empire: the Turks secured and protected the state militarily while commerce, industry and money-changing lay in the hands of the Greeks, Armenians and Jews. They kept the economic and social life going, and secured by their many-faceted activities the income for the Ottoman central administration which was so necessary to the state for its existence.

This distribution of labour – of course there were exceptions – corresponds to the difference in national characteristics and abilities of the two communities. The more deliberate, rural-oriented Turk preferred to opt for a steady wage in the civil service, while the more agile, risk-taking Greek in contrast preferred to remain independent and earn an income from commerce and industry.

With the conquest of Cyprus in 1570/71 settlers were brought in to colonize the island from the Anatolian mainland – a totally new element. These settlers, the ancestors of the Turkish Cypriots, made their living as farmers and civil servants. When the British took over control in 1878 this remained so. Significantly more Turkish than Greek Cypriots worked in the civil service. This no doubt came about too because the British could be sure of the loyalty of the Turks, whose concept of the state made them ideal civil servants. They see the state as the power which protects them and establishes order. For the Greeks on the other hand, with their strong sense of individuality, government is a necessary evil which makes them feel restricted and which they always approach with a sense of mistrust.

During the Ottoman times the Turks were not badly off, since in the final analysis they had the power and could skim off through taxation whatever might make the Greeks too powerful as a result of their commercial abilities. During British colonial times both Greeks and Turks played out their roles without revolt, since when it came down to it, they were both under foreign rule and the tone was set by the British.

The conflict was not to be avoided when in 1960 the economically stronger community, that is to say the Greeks, took over power. The constitution, which had previously been agreed upon, was meant to guard against this and worked out a system to take into account the existing structure and the national characteristics of both communities: so in the new Republic the Turkish Cypriots were given forty per cent participation in the army and the police and thirty per cent in the civil service, although they were only twenty per cent of the population. This was of course difficult for the Greek side to accept. Nevertheless Archbishop Makarios gritted his teeth and signed the agreements which led to independence. This was of course the second bitter pill that the Greeks had to swallow since they had fought against Britain not for independence, but for union with Greece.

Since the spring of 1955 when the Greek Cypriot EOKA fighters turned their struggle against their Turkish compatriots, a rift has developed between the two communities, which had previously co-existed peacefully for centuries. The terror of EOKA, and especially that of its fanatical leader, the ex-Greek army general George Grivas, was directed against the Turkish Cypriots because they stood in the way of the movement. As soon as it became clear that Grivas, in close cooperation with the Greek Orthodox Church and Archbishop Makarios, was less interested in freeing Cyprus from colonialism than in achieving Enosis, the Turkish Cypriots had to take the side of Britain, whether they wanted to or not.

For the Turks in Cyprus a continuation of colonial rule seemed preferable to becoming a minority in their own homeland once it was united with Greece, a minority which would have to fight for its very existence. In view of the recent tense and unpleasant experiences of Greeks

and Turks with each other and in view of the ineptness with which each respective majority has treated the minority, this fear of the Turkish Cypriots was not so far off the mark. So that during the years of struggle from 1955–58, which shook the island from the ground up, the Turkish Cypriots became the natural allies of the British – for which the Greeks have never forgiven them. Already in those years there were bloody inter-communal conflicts and one could see the outline for the present situation: a divided country and an island cut through the middle. For the Turkish Cypriot politicians, encouraged and supported by Turkey, countered the Greek idea of Enosis with their own concept – that of partition, "Taksim".

Anyone who looks through the archives or at old films for documentation of those years has an eerie feeling of how history develops into bitter reality despite all efforts to the contrary. One sees Turkish Cypriot demonstrators in 1956 or 1957 carrying placards showing the island divided and one also catches glimpses of a Cyprus completely swallowed up by Turkey. Emotions ran high on both sides, nevertheless both sides still thought in terms of a joint future even though from a different perspective. Each side thought itself to be in the right: the Greeks thought, relying on the principles of majority rule and self-determination, that they alone had the right to decide the future of the island, and that meant – as things stood then – the union of Cyprus with Greece. The Turks, on the other hand, wanted to preserve their rights and status, that is not to lose their homeland in Cyprus. In answer to the terror campaign of EOKA they created their own underground organisation TMT (the Turkish Defence Organisation) which was no less brutal when it struck. It was especially hard during those years for the few moderates on both sides who called for the common good and who could not see today's enemy in yesterday's neighbour and friends. Both EOKA and TMT took action against these "traitors" in their ranks and wiped them out without a second thought.

While everywhere else in the world the main forces in the fight against colonialism were working towards the same aim – decolonisation – in Cyprus right from the start the Greeks and Turks found themselves on opposing sides. The gap widened rapidly but one must also say that emotions were fanned by the politicians of both sides, often against the natural instincts of the simple man in the street.

The end result was neither Enosis nor Taksim. Great Britain, Greece and Turkey agreed to the independence of Cyprus through the Zurich and London agreements, by which they also undertook to guarantee the constitution and territorial integrity of the young Republic. The hurdles which this newly-created state had to overcome and the legacy of the years of bloodshed proved too great a burden, however. The Greek side did not want to accept the overproportional representation of the Turkish side in the state and administration and saw themselves being hindered in their economic activities by their slower neighbours. Even worse, within the Greek community there were many who criticised the Archbishop, who was also the newly-elected President, for having signed the agreements for independence and betraying the idea of Enosis.

Makarios himself did nothing to clarify the situation. As President he acted as the leader of an independent Cyprus, but as head of the church he continued to pursue the idea of Enosis, even when it was clear that this could not be achieved through political means. This discredited him with the Turkish Cypriots right from the start and undermined the foundations of the young Republic. For the Turks, who thought in the secular terms established by Atatürk and the strict separation of church and state, this unification of head of the church and state in one person was suspect from the very beginning. However, according to the constitution the majority community chose the President, and as Makarios was the undisputed leader of the Greek community the Turks had to accept what was, from their point of view, an absurd situation, that is to say a Christian Archbishop as President. They themselves elected the Vice-President.

The emotions on both sides were extremely tense. While the Greeks, in accordance with their temperament, immediately took the fate of this new polity into their hands and brought about the material development of the young Republic with their incredible talent for commerce and industry, the Turks remained on the sidelines and the economic development passed them by. It is pointless to speculate on whether the Greeks deliberately tried to keep the Turks in a disadvantageous position. It was definitely not in the nature of the Greeks to see their own respectable success and profits fall into the hands of the Turks. It is however equally true that the latter, due to their history and cultural development, find it more difficult to deal with questions of money, the accumulation of capital, economic expansion and the building up of commercial contacts. Since the differences between the two communities in this area were no longer camouflaged by British colonial rule, it now became clear that economic power was also the key to political power.

The constitutional conflict which now developed had its roots deep in the economic infrastructure of the island and this structure was not something which had been forced on the two communities, but which corresponded, and still corresponds today, to their natural characteristics. So that as long as this economic inequality between Greek and Turkish Cypriots continues, a real solution to the problem cannot be contemplated.

What applied then applies equally today: the Turks wanted to get rid of the Greeks' economic and political majority rule but were not able to get themselves into a position of equality. The Greeks, on the other hand, wanted the over-representation of the Turks in state and political institutions, through which they also felt their economic importance diminished, reduced to correspond with their true numerical proportion. In view of the discord within their own camp, they had neither the generosity nor the political maturity to win the Turks over to the common state by scrupulously respecting the rights given to them in the constitution. The Turks in turn blindly insisted on their rights and were not prepared to make any compromises or show any understanding. To mention only one example: from its foundation the state of Cyprus had to manage without an income tax law; the Greeks and Turks could not agree on this vital question. As Makarios then tried to change those paragraphs in the constitution which to the Greek side seemed unworkable, the Turks objected – as was to be expected. The extremists on both sides had long been preparing for another round. On the night of Christmas 1963 a

The north-west tower of the fortifications of Famagusta, probably Othello's Tower. Around 1878.

harmless incident lit the powderkeg. Makarios' enemies in his own camps saw the chance to achieve Enosis, to which he as head of the state had an ambivalent attitude, and they attacked the Turkish community, which defended itself bitterly. Civil war reigned again in Cyprus.

As a result of the bloodbath the unitary state collapsed. The Turks collected in enclaves at many points and inexorably expelled the Greeks. In many places Turkish employees and civil servants were not allowed access to their places of work, so the Turkish side pulled itself out of the joint power structure and set up its own administration in the enclaves. At this point in time both sides argued about legitimacy. The now purely Greek administration has remained the internationally recognised administration till today. The United Nations and the international community thus pay homage to the principle of majority rule.

Already during the unrest of 1963/64 British troops from the sovereign bases of Akrotiri and Dhekelia had sought to prevent the worst, and it is because of them that the "Green Line" – which divides the capital, Nicosia, into Greek and Turkish sectors – came about. The line was drawn with a green pen by an English officer as a dividing line between the two combatants, taking into account as much as possible the concentration of population of the two groups in each area of the town. Since then the Turks have forbidden the entry of all Greeks to "their" area of Nicosia.

The picture was similar in other parts of the island. The old Venetian Famagusta, which the Turks called Magoşa after the conquest by Lala Mustapha in 1571, had been purely Turkish ever since then. The Greeks had been driven out of the old part of the town and founded a new town outside the town walls: Ammohostos, which means "hidden in the sand". This small Greek town on the coast with its wonderful beaches became the nucleus of the tourist boom in Famagusta after independence in 1960. In Larnaca and Paphos too the Turks cut themselves off from the Greeks in their own part of the town – but in other places such as Limassol or Kyrenia, the Turkish parts of the town were open to all. Here the Greeks even patronised Turkish restaurants with their excellent cuisine.

Gradually everyday life came back to normal. Tens of thousands of Turkish Cypriots went back to work for the Greeks, particularly in the construction and tourist industries. In their own areas the economy was idle. A lack of organisational skill and capital, plus authorities to whom everything which was a prerequisite for economic development appeared foreign, were the real reasons for the stagnation on the Turkish Cypriot side. The economic blockade which the Greeks carried on for a while added to the difficulties.

People on both sides would certainly have recovered from the wounds of the past if the majority of the politicians had not continuously pointed them out. The intercommunal talks which were brought about under the auspices of the United Nations and carried on for years by the moderate Greek Cypriot President of the Parliament Clerides and the second man on the Turkish side Denktash, with a view to establishing a new constitutional order – that is, to provide a new start for Greek and Turkish Cypriots – raised hopes on both sides. The Cypriots were thoroughly fed up with the conflict, and the majority of Turks saw in addition that the irresistible economic boom on the Greek side would leave them more and more behind if a new order was not established.

On the Greek side, business success and political insight led people to see that Enosis, for which so much blood had been shed, would only damage Cyprus. People saw that even a small state could exist very well. The per capita Gross National Product was double that in Greece. Cyprus enjoyed international recognition, and her President Archbishop Makarios was one of the leading figures in the non-aligned movement. He was never tired of saying that he belonged to the West, but in his Byzantine way he often played the West off against the East. In short, Cyprus was often in the headlines of the world press and not only because of its internal problems. Union with Greece would mean that it would become an unimportant far-flung province of Greece, quite apart from the fact that Turkey would never allow this. At the end of 1973, the intercommunal talks had reached a breakthrough. A solution had been reached which took into account the most important demands on both sides: a proportional distribution of power, from the head of the state right down to local government posts at village level, with economic and financial concessions to the Turks. Both sides could have lived with this compromise because it settled the differences which had divided the two sides. This rapprochement was unquestionably brought about by the diplomatic skill of the two negotiators. The moderate pro-Western Clerides was always in favour of finding a solution with the Turkish community, otherwise Cyprus as a whole would have to pay for the mistakes of the past. Denktash, who was definitely the most far-sighted politician on the Turkish side, found himself under pressure from the opposition on his own side, who saw a modus vivendi with the Greeks as preferable to their ghetto-like existence.

Partition and its consequences

But things turned out differently, and the wheel of fate was once again set in motion. On the Greek side there was dissent over the agreement. Instead of putting it into action immediately Makarios wavered in the face of the hard line taken by those members of the community who had not learnt anything from the past. In the intervening years his former comrade from EOKA times, George Grivas, had turned into a bitter enemy. Grivas was now fighting with a new group, the secret organisation "EOKA-B" within the Greek community against the "traitor" Makarios, whom he accused of acting as head of an independent state instead of carrying out his ordained national duty to unite the island with Greece.

Once again, as so often in their history, the Greeks missed a unique political opportunity. Personal interests, the emotionally charged conflict between various groups and cliques overrode the reasonable element that called for compromise in order to save the integrity and sovereignty of the island at the last moment. The conflict on the Greek side was useful to the Turks. They pulled back from the agreement, an action which led many people to believe that Denktash was cleverly playing a double game. He was from the beginning, that is to say 1955

when the Greek struggle against the British started, a hardliner against compromise and for partition, the partition of Cyprus. Already in those early years he was prepared to go much further than the leader of the Turkish Cypriot community Fazil Kütchük, who became Vice-President of Cyprus in 1960. The reasons why this solution disintegrated are not clear, but now fate took over and even the UN troops, which had been stationed on the island since 1964, could not prevent it.

After months of continuous attacks by Grivas' supporters against Makarios and the institutions of the state, the tiny army, the National Guard, carried out a coup against the President on 15th July 1974. This had been preceded by significant differences between Makarios and the strong man of the Athens military regime, Ioannides. Ioannides was a fervent believer in Enosis, and the Cypriot National Guard was trained and led by officers from the Greek mainland. Makarios managed to flee from the Presidential Palace while it was under attack, but lost power and had to be rescued by British helicopters from the Akrotiri base and from there taken to New York via Malta and London. There he castigated Greece's attack on Cyprus' sovereignty before the United Nations Security Council as a breach of the Treaty of Guarantee over Cyprus, which Greece had also signed in 1960.

In the meantime Nikos Sampson, who had played such an infamous role during the EOKA times as a "Turk killer", a fanatic for whom there had always been only one aim, to free Cyprus from the Turks and make it part of Greece, was made President by the people behind the coup.

Turkey understandably saw this as a threat to her community even though during the bloody coup not a single hair on the head of a Turkish Cypriot was touched. The fighting took place between the opponents and supporters of Makarios and was thus restricted to the Greek side. The Turkish Prime Minister Ecevit tried personally in London to convince Great Britain to undertake joint action with Turkcy to re-establish constitutional order in Cyprus. But the British Government was not willing to do this, although it had also signed the Treaty of Guarantee as the third and most important power on the eve of Cypriot independence. And so

Turkey took the disastrous step alone. On the 20th July 1974, hardly a week after the coup against Makarios, it attacked the island with absolute superiority in the air and at sea, and with a highly equipped invasion force of about 40,000 soldiers. In three days of bitter fighting these troops secured a corridor from the harbour town of Kyrenia, where they landed, to the Turkish enclave in the northern part of Nicosia, even though on the same day, the 20th July the UN passed a resolution calling for an immediate cease-fire.

This was the first offensive war in Europe since the Second World War, and it took place within the Western camp: both Turkey and Greece, which had sparked off the Cyprus crisis, are members of NATO. Cyprus itself had remained non-aligned since its independence in 1960, but the stationing of Greek and Turkish troops on the island – which was written into the constitution – meant that two NATO forces faced each other as enemies here.

The Athens military regime collapsed under the shock and in Cyprus Sampson was replaced by the President of the Parliament Glafcos Clerides, who in accordance with the constitution was to act as President when the President-Elect could not do so. Makarios remained abroad as before. Up to this time most people would have seen the Turkish invasion of this unprotected island, cruel as it was, as understandable and defensible. This is the view of many politicians and to some extent is supported by international law. I shall never forget the conversation of a small group of journalists with a Turkish general at the old Crusader castle of St. Hilarion, which took place during these early days. From the castle one could see the whole theatre of war laid out like a chessboard, the bridgehead west of Kyrenia, the idyllic harbour town which had been bitterly fought over for three days, the wooded hillsides of Bellapais and Buffavento now blackened by napalm and bombing. "The Greeks invited us in," he said without flinching a muscle. And then he let the cat out of the bag. "This area which we have conquered will remain Turkish for ever, for ever." A British colleague found this so unbelievable that he answered the general, "You don't really believe that the world will allow it." But the general said only two words as he turned away, two words which hang like rocks over Cyprus, "for ever".

This makes it clear that the Turks did not only come to Cyprus to re-establish the constitutional order. The events which had made Europe hold its breath for four weeks, because as a consequence of the tragedy in Cyprus the possibility of war between Greece and Turkey looked imminent, showed clearly what Turkey's real intentions were. One Turkish ultimatum after another left Acting President Clerides, who was himself prepared to compromise but had little manoeuvreability in view of the inflamed feelings of the Cypriot people, with no way out. One kilometre after another the Turkish troops pushed forward while the participants at the Geneva Conference negotiated under this pressure. The Turkish side pushed their territorial demands as well as their political demands into areas which were no longer acceptable to the Greeks. After four weeks the army from the Anatolian mainland pulled its last punch: with over 300 tanks and supported by heavy air bombardments it broke through the corridor between Nicosia and Kyrenia which it had widened in the meantime to the east and west. For three days and nights Cyprus, the island of love and beauty, was suffocated by the dust raised by columns of tanks in the 40° heat, the roar of bombs and rockets, and by the pain and suffering of 200,000 Greek refugees who navigated their way through the fighting armies in an effort to reach the south, which had not yet been taken over by the Turkish army, and save at least their lives. Even today no-one knows how many lives were lost in this war. The figure of at least 5000 dead seems realistic. More than 2000 people, Greek and Turkish, are still listed as missing. In the wake of this conflict there were new massacres of unprotected Turkish Cypriots by the EOKA extremists. After three days Cyprus was divided, and all the efforts of the United Nations and the United States to change this situation have proved unsuccessful.

Archbishop Makarios returned to his post as President of Cyprus. In Cyprus as elsewhere in the world, his meeting at the beginning of 1977 with Rauf Denktash, who in the meantime had become the leader of the Turkish side and thus Makarios' opposite number, was seen as a sensation. They agreed on the outlines of a solution to the Cyprus question in terms of a federal, bicommunal, bi-zonal, non-aligned Republic. With the exception of non-alignment, which was not new and corresponded to Makarios' international policy, all the other aspects were con-

40

Continued on page 49

The priest of Phikardhou on his way to the village.

41

At prayer. In the Selimiye Mosque in the Turkish sector of Nicosia.

In many places women weave at home on their own looms.

Well-equipped. A shoemaker in his workshop.

The home of the puppeteer "Paphios" in Khlorakas near Paphos. The tradition of the shadow puppet theatre or Karagöz has survived in Cyprus till today. On the right, the wife of the artist.

The barber's shop is also the trading-place for local gossip.

Overleaf: a street café in Paphos.

Three generations of Cypriots.

cessions made by the Greek side, that is to say an acceptance of Turkish *faits accomplis*. Nevertheless Makarios had come to accept, though not without difficulty, the idea of a federal state made up of Greeks and Turks. This was a bitter pill for Greek public opinion when compared with the earlier concept of a unitary state with a clear differentiation between the majority and the minority. In accordance with the Turkish concept, this federation was not to be made up of a number of areas but of two regions only – the Turkish in the north – which had already in February 1975 declared itself the "Turkish Federal State of Cyprus" – and the Greek in the south. Each community would have equal rights, it would be a bi-communal state, with the Turkish Cypriots being accepted as equal partners. However the solution remained an outline only. The important questions as to how the constitution would look, what powers would be given to the central government and what to the federal chambers, what part of the northern area still held by the Turkish army would be given back, whether those refugees who wanted to return to their homes in the north – even under Turkish administration – would be allowed to do so, and whether those Turkish Cypriots who had been resettled by the Turks during 1975/76 in the north would be allowed to return to their villages in the south: all this remained open and unclear and still does today.

In August 1977, just half a year after the supposed breakthrough, Makarios died suddenly. This was a shock for the Greek Cypriots. His colourless successor Kyprianou, who has since then unsuccessfully handled the Cyprus question, has not to date managed to fill in the outline solution brought about by Makarios' charisma and political authority. In fact it is easy to see in the meantime that the victor of the long-drawn-out Cyprus crisis is Denktash, who stubbornly and uncompromisingly frustrates each new attempt to bring about an acceptable revision of the existing situation. He has no intention, in consensus with the interests of the Turkish army, of giving back the tiniest piece of the conquered area, which is around 38 per cent of Cyprus. He has not intention of letting even a fraction of the Greek Cypriot population back to their homes and villages. The resort town of Famagusta has remained uninhabited under Turkish control since the war, literally rotting in the hot, salty wind.

Denktash insists on the principle of equal representation of the two communities, that is, a fifty-fifty distribution of power in the form of a weak central government contrasted with far-reaching competence for the federal element in the future federation. He is fully aware that no Greek politician can accept these conditions and that time is on his side.

He was so sure of himself that in November 1983 he declared the north an independent state, so that the military *fait accompli* was consolidated politically. International efforts to find a solution to the problem, in which the West European countries, particularly those of the European Community, seem inexplicably unwilling to participate, have been set back by this manifestation of Turkish strength. The situation in Cyprus shows what the principle of self-determination really means today, the true weight of the United Nations, and how little they are able to do when one member state – Turkey – annexes almost half of another member state – Cyprus. The independent north of Cyprus has been declared illegal by the United Nations and is not recognised by any state other than Turkey, which controls it by troops stationed on the island and without which it would not be viable. The situation in Cyprus shows something else, however, which affects us Europeans: we are incapable of solving this totally European problem because we conduct our policies on the basis of the same double standards for which we are so ready to accuse the other side, that is to say the Eastern Bloc countries. What makes us – and by us I mean principally the European Community, of which Cyprus and Turkey are associate members and Greece in the meantime a full member – sit quietly by and watch while a majority is turned into a minority in Cyprus? By doing this, Europe is, in my opinion, abandoning one of the foundations of its democratic self-concept. It is giving in to the stronger side.

The partition of Cyprus in no way corresponds to the legitimate aims and desires of the Turkish Cypriots or the contractual and moral duty of Turkey to protect their security and existence. The Turkish Cypriots lived through difficult times in the years between 1955 and 1974, but have not come up with the winning ticket as a result of the events of 1974. If one looks closely, the people in the north of Cyprus are paying as high a price for the partition of the island as those in the south. Most of them do not really feel at home in their new surroundings. For the conservative rural element such changes are particularly difficult. Since time immemorial they have been cultivators of vines on the foothills of the Troodos mountains in the southwest, and now they must acquaint themselves with totally new agricultural methods in order to cultivate the citrus fruit and grain which predominate in the north. Many of the farmers still do not trust the political situation and so invest a minimum of energy and capital in their new piece of land, just enough to make a living. As all economic cooperation with the Greek side has come to a complete standstill, and since the Turks in the north are still far from being able to support themselves, they are dependent upon Turkey and its economy which is in a permanent crisis. This dependence becomes stronger from year to year, the more so since immediately after the partition in 1974 the Turkish lira was introduced as the currency of northern Cyprus and because the settlement of Anatolian farmers and shepherds – probably about 40,000 people, there are no reliable figures available – means a further step towards integration with Turkey. The presentiment that the north of Cyprus will at some time become the sixty-eighth province of Turkey simply because it is not capable of existing on its own, is in no way far-fetched. Since 1974 Turkey, though struggling to achieve its own economic recovery, has borne the whole burden of the budget for northern Cyprus, not to speak of the cost of stationing her troops there.

When the northern part of Cyprus was conquered in 1974 it contained about seventy per cent of Cyprus' national resources: the tourist goldmines of Famagusta and Kyrenia, the valuable citrus plantations all along the north coast with its plentiful water supply, the industry for the production of construction materials, the Mesaoria plain, "the land between the mountains" lying between Nicosia and Famagusta, the granary of Cyprus. Morphou with its springs and orchards in the northwest, and Famagusta in the east, at that time the only port for ocean-going vessels, provided equally important economic assets. All of these have since then been under Turkish control. And yet the economy is stagnating, for instance tourism is restricted almost entirely to Turks from the mainland, who bring no foreign exchange, only worthless lira.

The whole focus of the economy has moved from north to south in the short intervening period since 1974. Before 1974 who would have considered Ayia Napa, Limassol or Paphos when deciding where to have a holiday in Cyprus? One covered the south with a quick tour at the most. Who would have thought it possible before 1974 that the Greek farmers in the south would cultivate and export large quantities of such products as bananas, avocados and strawberries, fruits which did not exist in Cyprus earlier, while in the north army trucks carry away the dried-up citrus trees which have traditionally been cultivated in Cyprus, but nevertheless need constant and knowledgeable care, for firewood? Who would have expected that Cypriot construction companies, which are among the most active and successful of those working in the Gulf countries, would turn the south of the island into one gigantic building site while in the north, with all its potential for development, almost no progress can be seen? In view of these contrasting aspects of the island it is hard to believe that the one side lost the war in 1974 and that the other side won it.

So some Turkish Cypriots today look longingly at the other side. There is no-one in the north who wants to see the earlier political situation – which was one of fear and insecurity for the Turkish Cypriots – re-established. And there is no-one who believes that there is any workable solution for the future other than a federation of the two sides – this is the only way the Turkish Cypriots see their legitimate interests, and above all their security, as being guaranteed in the long run. However, there are many who do not want to travel the hard road to partition and the union of the north with Turkey. Opposition to the ambitious Denktash is strong. It is made up of the younger Turkish Cypriots who have picked up democratic – one could say social democratic and left-wing liberal – ideas during their education in England, whereas the circle in Turkey which Denktash uses as his base is right wing with military connections. This is the major anxiety of the opposition within the Turkish community: that they will have to live with the army from the mainland for an indeterminate period of time so

long as the division of Cyprus continues. And so these young intellectuals find themselves in a difficult situation. On the one hand they definitely do not want the re-establishment of Greek political control – and here they are at one with Denktash; on the other hand they themselves do not advocate a Turkish version of Enosis. They feel themselves first and foremost Cypriots, but in the face of the tens of thousands of new settlers from Anatolia they hardly have any chance to make their point.

There never was a common Cypriot identity or consciousness, and in view of the problems which faced the young Republic after 1960 there was no possibility for it to develop. Greeks and Turks are proud of their national traditions and it would be stupid to think that one could ever make them into one nation. Such a Cyprus will never exist. But what is still alive on both sides – and what provides the last chance for Cyprus – is an understanding of themselves as Cypriots which separates them from the Greeks and Turks of the mainland, that is to say from the Cypriots' point of view, in a positive way. This is the result of their colonial past: for Cypriots, Greece is too Balkan and Turkey too oriental.

The British set the administrative character of Cyprus and to some extent had an improving influence on both sides: the Greeks' sense of individuality was toned down by the principle of "common sense" and taking others into account, while Turkish sleepiness was vitalised. Even today one senses this British legacy. Authorities and administrative bodies are more reliable than elsewhere in the Mediterranean, corruption is rare, appointments are punctually kept, the shops close at exactly six o'clock, and as in England the society ladies go to their five o'clock teas, which are the most important social events for the exchange of gossip. Greek and Turkish Cypriots think of and travel to London first when they speak of Europe, and there are more Cypriots of Greek and Turkish origin living in London today than in the whole of Cyprus. By the Thames, incidentally, they get along well together and there are no problems there: the Turkish restaurateurs order their "haloumi", the piquant, rubbery cheese made from goat's milk, from their Greek colleagues along with wine and Cypriot brandy, a mild pure cognac without

52

*A country scene
in Peristerona (left),
and in a village
east of Kyrenia.*

*A building
in Neohorio (left).*

*Gossiping in
Phikardhou.*

53

which no Turkish Cypriot can exist. And Turkish Cypriots work in many Greek Cypriot establishments as cooks, accountants and drivers. Here the two communities complement one another in an ideal way, almost without friction, in a way which does not function back home. Why? "Here it is as if we still live under colonial rule as we used to in Cyprus," the owner of a successful Turkish restaurant in London explained to me once. "In England we both really have the same rights and duties, no-one asks 'are you Greek or Turkish?' We are Cypriots and don't forget, here there are no Cypriot politicians."

Many educated Cypriots studied in London after the Second World War. They think more along British lines than a Greek in Athens or a Turk in Ankara; one could say they think more like Europeans. In fact Cyprus is closer to Europe than Greece, let alone Turkey, and not only because of the mentality of its inhabitants. This island was always the most easterly outpost of Europe in the Mediterranean, and the European identity of its inhabitants is in continual conflict with their Greekness or Turkishness. This is exactly what is typical of the people of Cyprus and explains why both the Turkish Cypriots as well as the Greek Cypriots feel superior to their counterparts on their respective mainlands. There were and still are tensions which even resulted in bloody conflicts between the local Turkish Cypriots and the new colonists from east Anatolia, who were brought to Cyprus against the will of the Turkish Cypriots. These colonists come from the most backward areas of east Anatolia and are much less developed than the Turkish Cypriots, in whom British colonial thinking still remains rooted. The same can be said of the experts who were sent to rebuild the economy of northern Cyprus in the wake of the Turkish army. Their arrogance, which is not based on any visible achievement, has deeply offended the Turkish Cypriots. So the whole situation is not as harmonious as the politicians like to make it seem to outsiders.

The Greek Cypriots, too, have reached the conclusion that their brothers from the mainland have betrayed them. Cyprus was always a hotly debated subject in Greece's internal political scene. And the influence of Greece was almost always in play in one guise or another – either openly or camouflaged – when there was unrest, a crisis or catastrophe in Cyprus. The coup against President Makarios in 1974, which was inspired and directed from Athens and which brought about the Turkish invasion of Cyprus, is the clearest example. But Athens should have known that Cyprus cannot be held or protected from Greece. Turkey has all the strategic and logistic trump cards on her side. Turkish fighter planes can be over Cyprus in less than five minutes, whereas those from Greece need at least forty, and if they are then unable to land and refuel in Cyprus are thus cut off from returning even before they are involved in an air battle. Before Greek warships even reach Cyprus, Turkey could surround the Mediterranean island with her fleet and under its protection transport a whole army to Cyprus. A quick look at the map is enough to show how the next Cyprus crisis will end. Even though they do not readily admit it, many Greek Cypriots, especially the younger ones, are aware of their powerlessness; they will be helpless should a new round of fighting encircle the island. The adherents of the Turkish Cypriot leader Denktash, as well as the Turkish army, have never lost sight of their ultimate aim to make Cyprus a Turkish island. From Athens come the counter-slogans of a hellenic, totally Greek Cyprus, slogans which are disseminated in a warlike and fiery manner by the Greek Orthodox Church of Cyprus to counter the threat of Turkish Islamic expansion. The more thoughtful element in Cyprus sees the situation more realistically and not so one-sidedly, but the tone is set by those chauvinists who want to solve the Cyprus problem today with the nationalistic thinking of the 19th century. This converges with the involvement of outside interests which have been deciding Cyprus' fate for the last three thousand years.

The times change, the names and the kingdoms, but never the pattern: history is as timeless as fate. With Cyprus, an ancient tragedy is being written in our time and even beyond. St. Neophytos, who lived as a hermit in a cave near Paphos at the end of the 12th century and described and lamented the fall of Cyprus, spoke for the Cyprus of today as well: "The bad luck which oppresses our country hangs like mist over us." It looks as if only a miracle can help this beautiful island, which nevertheless at every turn produces evidence of some miraculous occurrence.

*The British Gover-
nor rides out of
Nicosia into the
country. Around 1880.*

Miracle upon miracle

One lands near Larnaca between the sea and the Salt Lake, which during winter and spring is home for swarms of flamingoes which migrate from the Caspian Sea to the warmer climate of Cyprus. Larnaca – the name is said to go back to the Greek word "Larnax" meaning sarcophagus, perhaps because there were supposed to be many of them scattered around the town, or was it perhaps a necropolis? Or does the unusual name have something to do with the death and resurrection of its patron saint Lazarus, who according to legend is supposed to have come to Cyprus from Palestine after his resurrection from the dead and to have spent his second life as the first bishop of the young parish of Larnaca? His grave with the inscription "Lazarus, the friend of Christ" was found at the end of the 9th century and the church which was built over it was named after him. The sarcophagus with the remains of his relics – many of which have been stolen and are venerated outside Cyprus – is to be found in the crypt of the church: Larnaca – Larnax – sarcophagus.

Another miraculous event took place by the Salt Lake a few minutes outside the town. As Lazarus, raised from the dead but tired and hungry after his journey from Palestine, went into the town, an old women saw him from her flourishing vineyard. She refused him a few thirst-quenching grapes on the grounds that the vineyard had not produced anything that year. So Lazarus punished the clever liar by turning the vineyard into a salt lake. Even today it is said that the farmers who gather the salt (this profitable monopoly belongs to the government of Cyprus) sometimes find the gnarled remains of vines. Larnaca, however, doesn't only play a role in Christian legends, but it is also important for Muslim pilgrims.

A mosque surrounded by a grove of dark green palms stands on a hill overlooking the lake, which dries up in summer and autumn. This is also connected to a miraculous event which took place during the Arab invasions of Cyprus in the 7th century. An aristocratic lady – in old accounts she is described as an aunt or foster-mother of the Prophet Mohammed – fell off her mount and broke her "alabaster neck". Umm Haram, as she was called, was buried here at the spot where she met her death.

55

Umm Haram was accompanying her husband during the invasion of Cyprus in 647 A.D. She was neither the aunt nor the fostermother of the Prophet Mohammed, but probably the aunt of his temporary secretary Anas ibn Malik, but she was close to the Prophet because she had supposedly helped him to get from Mecca to Medina. Pious Muslims believe that a huge stone brought by angels from Mecca to Cyprus was suspended over Umm Haram's grave for hundreds of years. Only later was it supported by two other column-like stones. During the Ottoman rule, the Turks erected a mosque over the grave in 1816 and covered the three stones with valuable material. The grave of Umm Haram is the fourth most holy place of pilgrimage for many Muslims after Mecca, Medina and the Dome of the Rock in Jerusalem. During the Turkish rule of Cyprus, passing ships would lower their flags out of respect for Umm Haram. The name Hala Sultan Tekke (Tekke = a shrine over a grave) by which it is known today stems from Turkish times. Possibly there was a monastery of Dervishes connected with the mosque for a while.

The angels also brought about another miracle which one can see a few minutes' drive away from the Tekke, again one recounted by the Christians. The mosaics in the village church of Kiti (this name comes from the biblical Kittim, the Kition of the Phoenicians and Greeks, and is the precursor of the name Larnaca) are supposed to have been made by the angels, they are so delicate and beautiful. The name of the church is Panayia Angeloktistos, which means "built by the angels". The mosaic in the dome of the apse is the oldest Byzantine mosaic preserved in Cyprus and shows Mary with the Christ Child between the Archangels Michael and Gabriel – perhaps a reference to the angels who created it? It belongs to the 6th or 7th century when Cyprus was a part of the Byzantine Empire.

Miracle upon miracle, the landscape lives directly through them, and the people – Christians and Muslims alike – feel themselves protected in this world of secrets, mysteries, dreams and hopes. These are just a few examples which one comes across in the space of an hour, but the same applies all over Cyprus. There is no monastery, no historical ruin, no rock in the landscape, no stream which is not surrounded by myths and legends. It is never possible to establish exactly

A well-earned rest.
In Neohorio (left).

The village priest
is still sought out
today to give
advice on personal
problems. In Troodos.

where the particular custom, belief or superstition originates – and that is what makes the island so attractive to the sceptical, enlightened European. The clues always peter out, names and legends are interchangeable and the religious and spiritual worlds melt into one: timeless Cyprus.

Ancient, heathen customs were taken over by Christianity, adapted and are even today practised. Functions of the old gods were taken over by Christian saints without interruption. Fear of the "evil eye" is a widespread phenomenon which both Greeks and Turks have in common and which goes back to heathen times. Almost everyone protects themselves with a black and white eye on a blue glass bead as an amulet, pendant or as a guardian over the front door. This glass eye protects against evil and harm which another can cause me and my house. One does not only find this belief in the villages, in secret it is held by almost everyone. And one particularly finds these customs living on in the Greek Orthodox Church, which still conforms to the practice of early Christian tradition. The village priest has taken the place of the heathen temple priest with healing powers, who also acted as a doctor and who influenced both body and soul equally.

Even today the villagers go to the "pappas" or priest with their small sorrows and fears, and in many places old men and women work secretly in a totally heathen tradition as healers. The village saints, descendants of the ancient spirits of trees and springs, are called upon and requested, with an offering, to give help with all physical and spiritual problems.

In every church one sees wax models of human limbs hanging from icons on a string: heads, legs, ears, limbs which are supposed to symbolise the stomach, kidneys or liver and – again and again on the island of love – hearts in all sizes. One donates to the saint the part of the body, in wax, which is to be healed. Women who long for a child buy a wax model of a baby which they place in the church. Later these effigies are used to make candles for the church. The size of the wax pieces allows one to judge the income of the donor, since pure beeswax was and is very expensive in Cyprus.

Even more puzzling is another custom I have only so far found in this form in Cyprus. Anyone who enters the church of Ayia Solomoni in the catacombs of Paphos, or the cave of the hermit Agapitikos (which is now partly exposed due to erosion), will notice something which can also be seen out in the open next to a shrine or chapel: trees or bushes are covered with handkerchiefs or other articles of clothing knotted onto the branches till they are bleached by the sun and the wind and become bizarre tatters. Children's underwear, sleeves of shirts, all sorts of bits and pieces are to be found, and over and over again handkerchiefs, sometimes hundreds of them on a single bush. Usually this means that there was an ancient cult carried on here where people came in search of healing.

Today these places are linked with Christian saints. So a sick person makes a pilgrimage there to confide in a saint who is usually only responsible for a particular illness. Often he lights a candle and cuts off a piece of his clothing, but usually he parts with his handkerchief. Just as I separate myself from this piece of clothing I would like to be separated from my illness, that is all the custom means.

Anyone who comes across a village church "tied up" with cord is witnessing a similar phenomenon. Often holy shrines which can no longer be identified, or the graves of saints, are fenced off with long threads in such a manner. Angry spirits which spread an illness in the district are supposed to get caught up in the threads and the unholy is thus contained.

Many of the cults, which often went into the realm of magic, were connected with love or other emotions. Anyone who took earth from the floor of the cave of the hermit Agapitikos, "the one who achieves love", and put it in the drinking water of the beloved could count on his feelings being returned.

Agapitikos' cave neighbour was Misitikos. With some earth from his cave one could let the other person feel one's hate – Misitikos, "the one who achieves hate". Today Agapitikos' cave, open to the street on two sides, is always decorated with flowers. Bottles of olive oil stand next to lighted candles. And again and again it draws a young woman up the narrow path to quiet contemplation.

Everything which has to do with love in Cyprus goes back to Aphrodite, the Goddess of Love of ancient times. Her cult, the details of which we know little even today, was celebrated in Paphos. Not in the Paphos of today, which has only been known as Paphos since Roman times, but in Old Paphos where the temple of Aphrodite stood next to the little village of Kouklia. The foundations have been excavated. This was, if you like, the heart of ancient Greek Cyprus. It did not beat in the seven – or, according to some versions, ten – city kingdoms which divided the island, it beat here where the uncrowned queen of Cyprus ruled. From all corners of the ancient world pilgrims travelled here to take part in the mysteries. There were supposed to have been orgiastic flower festivals to honour the goddess who was so beautiful that her indescribable beauty could only be reproduced by a conical stone standing in the middle of the temple. One can see a reproduction of this stone on a coin from the time of Trajan, a coin which was minted in Paphos and which bears the inscription: league of Cypriots. Today it is part of the collection of the museum in Nicosia.

A black conical stone which came to light during the excavations in Old Paphos is also in the museum. No-one knows if it is the stone of Aphrodite, much less what went on around it. There was definitely something like temple prostitution because this is reported in many ancient sources. Each woman had to give herself to a stranger, a pilgrim, once in her life. And there was also the introduction of young men to the ways of love by experienced priestesses. The great feast of the goddess, who was also a goddess of flowers, was a spring festival, a celebration of fertility in which young and old took part with enthusiasm.

Not far from the temple there is a huge boulder in the sea, surrounded by smaller rocks. This is the spot where, according to the mythical legend, Aphrodite was born out of the foam of the sea and came onto land. But less attractive figures also came onto land in this area during the history of Cyprus; the Saracens and Crusaders, the English King Richard the Lionheart and Turkish admirals, the British troops which took over Cyprus in 1878, and the fanatic fighter George Grivas who took it back from them.

Aphrodite's birthplace is today known as Petra tou Romiou, "the rock of the Greek". This links the spot with the Byzantine hero Dighenis, who fought bitterly against the Arabs as they overran Cyprus. It is said that he threw the rocks, which today give the place its unusual appearance, into the sea out of anger at the disgrace. His mythical name was taken over by Grivas, who was everywhere and nowhere, as he launched his guerrilla war from the Troodos mountains to achieve "Enosis", the last expression of the Byzantine idea, the union of all areas settled by Greeks and with a Greek culture, into one state.

Makarios, dominant figure in politics and the church

Grivas "Dighenis" and Makarios, who in a way embodied the idea of Enosis and as Archbishop and President will go down in the history of our century as the last Byzantine, remained in the end unhappy figures. They came to a parting of the ways as Makarios, in 1959/60, realised instinctively that times were changing and came to accept the compromise solution of an independent Cyprus rather than the Greek Byzantine concept. At that time Makarios, by signing the London agreements, which were literally dictated to him, was able to prevent the catastrophe. Grivas, in his unthinking political blindness, would have brought Cyprus to the brink of disaster – a disaster which then in 1974 hit the island with the full force of history.

Makarios – the son of a farmer from the village of Pano Panayia, the novice at the richest and most influential monastery, Kykko, the young priest in Athens and Boston, the Bishop of Kition (Larnaca), and finally in October 1950 at the age of only 37 the Archbishop of the autocephalous Greek Orthodox Church of Cyprus – was born Michael Mouskos and chose for himself the name Makarios III. He became the spiritual leader of the resistance against the British and did not for an instant lose sight of the national longing for union with Greece as he carried out his Byzantine-style political plans. He managed, laughing affably, to win over even his sharpest critics and to cleverly keep from power the strong political force in Cyprus, the Communist party AKEL, whose Moscow-line policies are supported by about a third of the Greek Cypriot voters. His successor Kyprianou, on the other hand, had to enter into an alliance with the Communists in order to get himself elected in the last Presidential elections in 1983.

Makarios carried on international politics between East and West, between the Americans and the Russians, between NATO and the Warsaw Pact, and between Greece and Turkey. But in the last analysis he had to admit to himself, after the coup in 1974, that he himself had become a victim of this Byzantine labyrinth, into which he had been sending both his friends and his adversaries for so many years. In the end he stood alone without friends either in the West or the East. No-one lifted a finger to help Cyprus when the catastrophe hit the island. And till today criticism of the partition is only a verbal formality. Makarios never wanted to commit himself fully, so he fell in the end and Cyprus fell with him. He manipulated more artfully than some of the greatest figures of his time, but nevertheless throughout his life he remained trapped in the stubborn thinking of the Orthodox Church. Their elitist desire for leadership had no place for the Turkish Cypriots, who were and remained for the Church the infidels who had caused the fall of Constantinople and the Byzantine Empire and who also sought to kill Cyprus' Greek character, her soul: an ancient historical conflict but still as alive today as in 1453 when Sultan Mehmet the Conqueror entered Constantinople.

Other facts have been erased from the Greek Church's view of history: it was the Turkish conquerors who freed the Orthodox Church from the hated yoke of the Church of Rome when Cyprus became part of the Ottoman Empire in 1570/71. It was not the Greek churches which were turned into mosques, but the cathedrals of the Lusignan and the chapels of the Venetians. It was the Turkish sultans and governors who recognised the Archbishop as the Ethnarch, the national leader of the Greek community, a role which nurtured a man like Makarios with his undisputed moral and secular authority.

Island of contrasts

The relations between the Greeks and the Turks were not always as they are today. For many years they lived together even though, due to the mistrustful attitude of both religions, they kept a certain distance. At every turn one comes across the splendour, the tribulations and the moods of the history of Cyprus. Time and the various cultures have left so much behind on this island, which has a coastline of about 780 kilometres and which one could drive round in a day at West European speeds if one did not keep coming up against the unnatural borders, so that one needs a whole lifetime to get to know Cyprus. An island of contrasts, of unexpected encounters, criss-crossed with the footprints of our own and other people's history.

Here we find the foundations of the beehive house of Khirokitia, which go back eight thousand years and which represent the evidence of the first organised human life on the island, and a short drive away, the splendid hotels for tourists on the Limassol coast – hotels which are so comfortable and luxurious that they should survive into the next century. Along the Green Line in Nicosia barricades made of oil-barrels full of bullet holes, burnt-out cars and sandbags barely divide the streets across which Greeks and Turks used to talk to each other. At the tip of the 1951-metre high Chionistra (chilblain) also known as Mount Olympus, the highest peak of the Troodos mountains, stands the conical monitoring station with which the British and Americans can listen in over the sea and mountains right to the depths of the Soviet Union and the crisis areas of the Gulf.

On the white, hot sands of Ayia Napa, which especially attract Scandinavian and German tourists, the Cypriots have accepted that the ladies from the north go topless – but if one manages the winding road up to the monastery of Stavrovouni, one comes up against an iron door guarded by an unfriendly monk and a sign which has recently forbidden the entry of women to the monastery. Contrasts, contradictions, often extreme opposites to which every visitor to Cyprus can add his own examples.

60

Continued on page 69

The remains of the Bedestan in the Turkish quarter of Nicosia. In the background, the minarets of the Selimiye Mosque.

The 16th century icon from the Church of Ayii Anargyri in Phini, showing the Last Judgement, is now in the Byzantine Museum in Nicosia

The frescoes in the Church of Panayia Phorviotissa at Asinou are among the most important examples of painting from the Middle Ages in Cyprus. The Christ Pantocrator fresco dates from the 14th century.

An icon showing the Holy Virgin (14th/15th century), from Asinou Church, in the Byzantine Museum in Nicosia (left).

Another example of the collection of icons in the Byzantine Museum in Nicosia, Christ giving a Benediction, from the church Panayia tou Arakos in Lagoudhera. End of the 12th century.

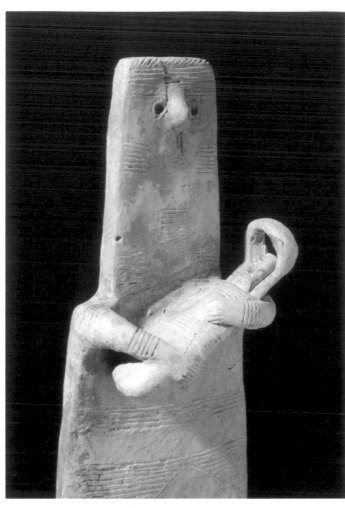

Terracotta figures from the Cyprus Museum in Nicosia: mother with child, from the early Bronze Age, around 2150–1850 B.C. (top left). Unique representation of a rider from the middle to late Bronze Age, after an Aegean prototype. Around 1300 B.C.

A male figure dating from 700–400 B.C. A votive figure showing Phoenician influence. 700–600 B.C. (lower right).

The famous marble statue of Aphrodite from Soli is among the best-known exhibits in the Cyprus Museum in Nicosia.

Friday prayers in the Selimiye Mosque, formerly St. Sophia's Cathedral, in the Turkish quarter of Nicosia.

"Why have you never been away from Cyprus?" I once asked a friend who had had many opportunities to do so. "Why should I travel?" was the answer. "We have the whole world here, the beauty of Cyprus lies in the variety of its landscapes." The somewhat worn-out catchphrases such as "the bridge between East and West" or "the crossroads of Asia, Africa and Europe" take on form and content when one actually experiences Cyprus. The face of the island is so varied that one can only describe it as a cosmos. And this is one of the reasons why it is so popular as a tourist resort: here there are enough worlds into which one can escape from the concrete jungle of tourism which – since 1974 – Cyprus can do without even less than previously. All this sometimes goes past like a series of slides, mosaic stones which only lead one to a total picture of Cyprus when they are taken together. No single one alone is characteristic of Cyprus.

There are the raw, naked rocky coasts near Paphos covered with luxuriant banana plantations reminiscent of the Caribbean, and a few moments later one finds oneself in a Mediterranean scrub landscape of thistles, shrubs and stones, surrounded by herds of sheep and goats. Then again there are white slopes covered with vines cascading down the mountainside in straight lines, millions of them it seems. Behind a village reminiscent of the Provence, an abrupt change: stretches of fields, a rich green colour in spring, tightly bound around with low stone walls which could be in the Ardennes or in England. High above on the ridge, gnarled, bare rocks loom darkly over the green fields; a small massif which recalls Scotland. On the way from Nicosia to Larnaca the strangely-shaped table mountains, flat on top, looking as if the surrounding desert had sunk and left these surfaces hanging in the air, shimmering in their whiteness.

The Mesaoria plain, the land lying between the Kyrenia mountains and the Troodos range, which is covered in spring with poppies and anemones, an endless meadow for Aphrodite, which changes in a few weeks by the end of May, when the corn is high and ripe, to the colours of autumn, and then again after the harvest towards the middle of June turns into the landscape of the steppes: Asia in Cyprus. The bewitching scent of the orange blossom near Morphou, Famagusta and Limassol contrasts with the heavy red earth of the British base in Dhekelia where the Cypriot farmers grow the biggest and tastiest early potatoes in the world. Pentadaktylos, "the five finger mountain", which looks as if it had been taken straight out of the Dolomites, swathed in legend, the most distinctive landmark on the Kyrenia range, and at its feet Kythrea, a unique garden of flowers watered by an inexhaustible spring from which Nicosia once drew its water: the Romans built an aqueduct here and took the water as far as Salamis, fifty kilometres away. In the 17th century the cauliflower was brought from here to Europe, and the water which flows from the spring and supports this lush vegetation (the Turkish name for the area, Degirmenlik, is a reference of the many mills in the district) is supposed to flow under the sea from the Taurus mountains in Anatolia.

The Tekke near Larnaca shimmers in the midday sun like an oasis: when the wind blows from North Africa bringing the red Sahara sand with it one feels as if one has been put down in another continent. High up in the Troodos mountains, two villages picked at random which are nevertheless special: one is Greek and can be reached from Kykko monastery by a narrow asphalt road from the north. It hangs onto the steep mountainside and boldly straddles the ridge like a saddle. The other used to be Turkish but is today inhabited by Greek refugees from the north. Children noisily play football in front of the mosque which has been nailed shut, in the coffee shop the Turkish inscriptions have still not quite faded away – a small asphalt road leads here as well, but this time from the south of the island. Between these two neighbours – who always kept at a certain distance but who, in recent years, found themselves at an anxious, watchful distance – no road was needed. Only a forest path leads through the valley, at some points merging with the river bed. Sunken paths, in spring a bubbling stream – this is as idyllic as the Black Forest. High above, the lush vegetation of tropical-type trees weaves itself into a vaulted hall with sunlight slanting through the windows, and yellow and black orioles shoot out of the arrow-like reeds, startled even by a slowly moving car, only to disappear again into the darkness of the moist greenery.

The beauty of Cyprus lies in the variety of its landscapes. But these landscapes would hardly be so full of depth and resonance if evidence of the different epochs and cultures were not sprinkled everywhere like flowers in a meadow: memories of the various peoples with which the inhabitants of the island live. The theatres of Salamis and Soli, stony shells on the coast of Cyprus. The tiny, inconspicuous churches crouching on the side of a mountain or the edge of a forest as if they did not want to be noticed, the interiors of which are covered with Byzantine frescoes. The eleven-spiked star of the Venetian walls with their bastions which still today mark off the old town of Nicosia, perhaps the most impressive stone composition in Cyprus. Inside the walls, as in Famagusta where the names Othello, Marc Antonio Bragadino as well as Lala Mustapha and Djamboulat Bey seem as fresh as those in yesterday's paper, are the Gothic cathedrals dating from the rule of the French House of Lusignan, where the Lusignan were crowned "Kings of Cyprus and Jerusalem". Cathedrals which remind one of those on the Loire when one enters them – but which are today mosques. The minarets, which look as if they had been clipped on, are evidence of the changing times and the change of power in Cyprus. Inside, under Gothic arches which have been whitewashed and covered with expensive carpets, pious Muslims say their Friday prayers: a clash of two worlds or an allegory of the fact that the extremes in the end eventually merge into one another.

One can interpret it as one likes: what cannot be disputed is that Cyprus reminds us Europeans of the history that formed us and rekindles all the old anxieties. Time has stood still here, one thinks at first. Only later does one realise that this is not exactly correct. Time has also moved on in Cyprus, but the people of the island have never cut themselves off from the past as we have done in the hectic West. They have simply taken it with them. And kept it with them. It is part of them. This is the most distinctive feature of Cyprus.

And this is exactly why the problem which today so depresses the Cypriots cannot be solved in the way in which we would solve it: with the green line of an English officer's pen on a map of Nicosia, or with an appeal to economic reason. Cyprus is not a museum in which one can just rearrange the legacy of centuries. Cyprus is living history.

Out of the many images which reflect the splendour and complexity of this island, for me one – perhaps the quietest – speaks the loudest: in a niche in the remains of the walls around the Temenos, the holy area of the temple of the Goddess of Love Aphrodite in Old Paphos, someone has placed a bundle of wild, now wilted, roses and next to them an apple, a piece of bread, a half-burnt candle. Cyprus – unity of time and place.

On the History and Culture of Cyprus

Proverbs

Friday's laughter becomes Saturday's tears.
Nothing spreads faster than gossip and a forest fire.
Work is hard, no work is harder.
There are no sparks in last year's ashes.
The son of the priest is the grandson of the devil.
If the stone falls on the egg – alas for the egg.
If the egg falls on the stone – alas for the egg!
Be content with your lot, even if you are a priest.
Once for a friend,
twice for a friend,
but not a third time.
Much talking is good only for scholars.
He who has a tree has shade.
Buy a shoe in your own country even if it be mended.
A rich man is like a lemon, the more you squeeze,
the more you get out of him.
A fool throws a stone into the sea and a hundred wise men cannot pull it out.
Send a fool and go after him.
There is no borrowing a sword in wartime.
If the baby doesn't cry, mother won't suckle.
The walls have ears and the fences eyes.

Folk songs

Mother, send me to get water,
fresh from the well.
And if it's not fresh
I won't enjoy my youth any more.

**Mother, send me
to get water**

      Mother, I reached the spring
      and filled my pitcher.
      Then suddenly I stumbled
      and my pitcher broke.

Daughter, tell me the truth
because the whole village already knows.
You didn't stumble,
a young man embraced you!   (Greek)

When I am dead

When I am dead
bury me in the market square
so that people can say,
"Oh, poor man!"

(Greek)

When I am dead
bury me in her yard
so that she can come and water me
like her lemon trees.

**The song
from Karavas**

By the river lie my clothes
in Nicosia my weapons
but my love lies in beautiful Karavas!

Orange tree of Karavas,
laden with oranges,
how many nights have I slept
in your arms!

Orange tree of Karavas, good night!
I was with you till dawn
and will be back another night!

(Greek)

The wedding song

During the preparation of the wedding meal "Resin" made of wheat and lamb:
"An eagle flies high in the sky
and a shadow falls on the girls
as they prepare the resin."

Sewing the bridal mattress:
"Put the four crosses on the four corners
so that the bride and groom
can sleep like turtle doves."

Dressing the bride:
"Today the sky is black.
A black day today
when child is separated from mother.
Call her father to put on her belt,
to give her his blessing and give her away."

Shaving the bridegroom:
"Oh, St. Andreas, who lives by the sea,
come and help the bridegroom to put on the bridal crown."

For the newly-weds:
"These two who are dancing here are a couple,
one is the sun, the other the moon.
May they live a long life together
and never want for wheat and oil."

(The Greek wedding song is sung during the preparations for the wedding, with usually the whole village taking part.)

Giving birth in the seated position, as was customary until recently in the villages of Cyprus. A clay figure from the 11th–4th century B.C. Cyprus Museum, Nicosia.

Two lullabies

Sleep soundly, my child
I've ordered your dowry in Polis,
your clothes in Venice,
and your weapons in Nicosia.

Sleep, which comes to children,
come and take this child too.
I give him to you a baby,
give him back to me an adult.

(Greek)

**Sleep soundly,
my child**

If you should come to Kyrenia
don't enter the walls.
If you should enter the walls,
don't stay long.
If you should stay long,
don't get married. If you should get married,
don't have children.

(Turkish)

**If you should
come to Kyrenia**

She wrapped her flesh in raiments which the Hours
And Graces made and dipped in springtime flowers,
All that the Hours bring forth. Crocus they bring,
Bluebell and violet brave blossoming.
Roses with lovely buds and nectarious scent,
Ambrosial petals of the jonquil blent

**Goddess of flowers,
Aphrodite**

With lily-cups. So Aphrodite wore
Clothes that the scent of every season bore.

STASINOS, *a Greek poet of Cyprus living in the 8th or 7th century B.C. From "Kypria Epi" (Songs of the Cypriot Heroes)*

Oracle

And then a great and celebrated singer
will be born
in sea-girt Cyprus
whom Themisto
the best of the best
will bear.
Her offspring born
in a lone, barren field
far from the fertile lands of Salamis,
will leave Cyprus behind
and over the waves
to great Greece will go,
and of her fate's black threads
be the first to sing a divine song which will cause him
not to age when he grows old
and not to die when he dies.

EUCLOS, *a Greek poet of Cyprus in the 8th or 7th century B. C., possibly a contemporary of Homer whose birth in Cyprus he foretells in this oracle. The birth of Homer in Cyprus is not historically substantiated.*

A hundred words of love

One, said the beauty, and he answered: I have eaten one of the love-cakes that you baked and now I am your slave.

Two, said she, and he answered: two pigeons with silver wings were playing, I saw how they kissed and thought it was us.

Three, said she, and he answered: Holy Trinity, let this girl love and kiss me so that the devil doesn't get me.

Four, said she, and he answered: a cross hangs around your neck and its arms caress your bosom.

Five, said she, and he answered: I sharpened five knives for you and I will pierce my heart with them in order to put an end to my pain.

Six, said she, and he answered: look at the Pleiades, they are six stars and the one who has no love is searching for them.

Seven, said she, and he answered: my love wanders about the seven planets in the sky but at night she is back in my arms.

Eight, said she, and he answered: the crab has eight legs and goes backwards. I have only one love and cannot kiss her.

Nine, said she, and he answered: your mother carried you for nine months like a flower, she nourished you so that you could share my bed.

Ten, said she, and he answered: just call out the tens so that I can keep up. Otherwise there are too many numbers and I may forget something.

Twenty, said she, and he answered: my twenty fingers and toes shake like leaves when you stand before me.

Thirty, said she, and he answered: Kassia with thirty branches through which the wind rustles, how I have loved you, my heart is consumed by love for you, who are as white as snow.

Forty, said she, and he answered: he who has hunger and fasts for forty days, can be revived with just one kiss.

Fifty, said she, and he answered: for fifty days i searched the halls of the castles in Venice for ivory combs and golden thimbles for you.

Sixty, said she, and he answered: there are sixty minutes in an hour and the whole house from attic to cellar hangs on your words.

Seventy, said she, and he answered: till you give me a kiss and we can love one another.

Eighty, said she, and he answered: even if they dig my grave eighty metres deep my soul will still protect you.

Ninety, said she, and he answered: even if I lie next to you for ninety years I will never get bored; should ninety years go by without my lying next to you I will never find sleep.

A hundred, said she, and he answered: I own the hundred keys to paradise and I will open the door to whoever kisses me first.

Go servants, and prepare the bridal bed, sprinkle it with musk and aloe and give us basilicum for love pillows.

A Cypriot folk song from the Middle Ages which says that only he who can recite the hundred words of love can win his beloved.

In Cyprus

I was not a little surprised when I spotted, shortly after disembarking, an elegant English coach, a vehicle which I had not seen for many a year. I was even more surprised when a European came up to me and invited me to take lodging with the local English Consul, Mr. Turner. The Consul's secretary who greeted me was called Mariti and later became well-known, even famous, for his book "Viaggi per l'isola di Cipro".

Larnaca lies at a latitude of 34° 35″ according to my observations. About half the population is made up of Mohammedans who have two impressive mosques for their religious practices. The Franciscans and the Capucines also have churches here which are frequently used by those orientals who are followers of the Roman Church. The climate of Larnaca was once extremely unhealthy and numerous inhabitants were carried off by an unpleasant fever. Impure drinking water was the cause. The inhabitants of the town can thank Bekir Pasha for the improvement. He built an aqueduct from the village Arpera to Larnaca and Saline and had the surrounding swamps filled in. […]

[…] In the whole of the Turkish Empire there is no province where the inhabitants are so repressed and exploited as those on the island of Cyprus. After the conquest there were 80,000 Greeks who had to pay the Charadsch (poll-tax). This tax was so high that many families were wiped out and therefore obliged to leave their homeland and seek homes elsewhere. Many became Mohammedans in order to avoid this poll-tax. The Turks nevertheless did not bother to question whether the population of Cyprus was shrinking or not, they still demanded the income which they had received from the first. All those who remained Christians had to pay the tax for those who had deserted, the well-off had to pay the tax for the poor. And then, as the Sultan gave a portion of the income which he received to the Vizier as a salary, the position of the Cypriots became even worse. Because no Vizier stayed here long. When a new one came, the inhabitants had to pay double because the new one was of the opinion that he did not have to worry what his predecessor had received. So it came about that the oppressed took up arms against the tyrant. Revolts became more and more frequent and when one of the Viziers demanded the poll-tax from the Mohammedans as well, all the inhabitants united regardless of religion, murdered the Vizier and set his palace on fire. After that the Sultan sent warships to Cyprus, a Pasha with the rank of two horsetails was commanded to put down the rebellion of 3000. But the rebels were in a castle in the north of the island and the Pasha was unable to conquer it. Only after he managed to lure the leaders out of the castle by a ruse was he able to put down the rebellion. Almost all the rebels were executed or sent into slavery. […]

[…] The most important products of the island of Cyprus are wine, silk, cotton, wool, wheat and barley. But since the number of inhabitants keeps decreasing, over the years production has become less and less. Very near Larnaca is a salt lake with a rich yield. Ships take this salt with them when they do not get any other cargo in Cyprus.

CARSTEN NIEBUHR, *the only survivor of the Danish expedition to the Yemen (1761–1767) visited Cyprus on his return journey. The surveyor from Friesland recorded his impressions in his book "Discoveries in the Orient" ("Entdeckungen im Orient")*

Cyprus wine
[…] The villager who sells the wine must see that it maintains its condition, whether it remains in his hands or is stored by the purchaser, up to August 15 next after the vintage. On that day it is examined, if it is spoiled the seller must take it back, if it is good it is charged to the buyer, for after the first year it is not subject to deterioration.

The island produces annually 40,000 couzai of wine (an old measure, a couza equals about ten litres). The whole crop takes its name from the "Commandery", which hardly supplies 10,000 couzai, but of the best quality. The rest comes from different parts of the island. Most of it is exported to Venice, where, even in the cafés, it is largely drunk. But the Venetians are not very particular about the quality, never buying wine more than 18 months old, and paying only a piastre the couza. The older or finer quality is sent to France, Holland and Tuscany, and costs from 2 1/2 to 3 piastres the couza. Of late a considerable quantity of the commoner wine has gone to Leghorn (Livorno, in Italy). It is exported in casks of 70 couzai: the tariff charges, including the value of the cask, amount to 10 3/4 piastres. The oldest wines in the market are eight or ten years old: it is not true as some people in Europe think, that one can find it of a hundred. It is customary however on the birth of a child for the father to bury a jar full of wine well sealed, which is kept until the day of his or her marriage, when it is served at the wedding feast, and distributed among relations and friends. This is the oldest wine one can find, and would be twenty years old or a little more; but it is never sold, being kept for presents.

The monastery of Stavrovouni
[…] On the summit is a church dedicated to the Holy Cross, built by St. Helena after her return from Jerusalem. A convent of Greek monks adjoining it is partly destroyed, but still gives an idea of its former size and solidity. In the church is preserved a fragment of our Saviour's Cross, as long as half a finger, and as thick as one's thumb. In later years doubt has been thrown on this relic, and this is the reason. Some Greek priests of the village of Lefcara conceived the idea of robbing the convent of so remarkable a relic to glorify their own church by its presence, and framed a cunning tale that a similar piece of the True Cross had been lately presented to them, which they wished to compare with that on the mountain, whose authenticity they knew to be indisputable, as it had come from the hands of St. Helena herself. These wily Lefcariots received permission to do so, and went over to the mountain with a sham relic so fashioned as exactly to resemble the true. When the two pieces were brought together they began to shuffle them about, and to wrangle over them, until at last no one knew which was the piece of the True Cross, each party claiming that honour for their own. The people continue to have more faith in that on the mountain, but frequent also the feast held at Lefcara; for opinions are divided, and to this day disputes and quarrels agitate the priests of the two churches. […]

The town and fortress of Kyrenia
[…] The town and fortress of Cerines (Kyrenia) are about 20 miles distant from Nicosia. The town is thinly peopled. The schismatic (Orthodox) Greeks, who make up the Christian population of the island, have a church there, the seat of a bishop, and the Turks a mosque. The government is administered by a commissioner and a judge. The inhabitants till the surrounding country, which gives a good return for their labour, for its many springs make this

The monastery of Stavrovouni near Larnaca was founded by St. Helena. Around 1880.

one of the most fertile districts in Cyprus. It produces wheat, barley, silk, cotton, oil and carobs; of the last whole shiploads are sent every year to Alexandria.

[…]

The castle of Cerines is built on the seashore upon a rock: its foundation is clearly coeval with that of the ancient city, but it was enlarged by the Lusignan Kings. Europeans are not allowed to enter it, and the Turks look angrily at anyone who comes too near its walls. I was allowed to study them, and even to enter the ditch which surrounds them. It is one of the best preserved forts which I have seen in this part of the world in the hands of the Turks. The castle is now in some places out of repair; and it is even said that the Sultan has given orders for its destruction, which have not been carried out.

Close to the fort is a harbour, or rather a basin, just large enough for two or three small vessels. It is the point of embarkation for Caramania (an area on the Turkish mainland opposite); the passage is made in seven or eight hours. It is a great convenience to the island to receive frequently by this route letters from Constantinople and Europe generally: two French boats are constantly employed on this service. Other vessels which trade with this side of the island, especially for carobs, stand out to sea about three miles. The landing is bad, and only possible in summer. From the shore near Cerines the Caramanian mainland is visible; lights can be seen across the strait, and are used as signals to the boats, when there are passengers waiting and both boats are on the same coast.

ABBÉ GIOVANNI MARITI, *who is mentioned as the Secretary of the Consulate by Carsten Niebuhr, filled this post in Cyprus from 1760 to 1767. He worked in the English Consulate in Larnaca, which also represented the interests of the Danes, the Dutch and citizens of Tuscany. Giovanni Mariti is one of the few chroniclers of the daily life and history of Cyprus who only recorded what he had actually seen with his own eyes or what he could prove via reliable witnesses. Many others based their reports on what previous travellers or chroniclers had recorded.*

The next morning at dawn the city was attacked at all points. This assault lasted six hours, with very little loss on our side, for the Turks fought with less spirit than usual. They kept giving us great trouble on the seafront with their galleys, firing at every attack, and battering every part of

The sixth attack

the city which they could reach. This assault was warded off, but the city was reduced to great straits, only seven barrels of powder were left, so the chiefs resolved to surrender under honourable conditions.

On August 1, when noon was passed, a truce was made, and an envoy came from Mustafa Pasha, with whom it was agreed that the following morning two hostages should be given on either side while the agreement was under discussion. By order of the right worshipful Bragadino there went out as hostages on our side Count Hercole Martinengo, and Signor Matteo Colfi, a citizen of Famagusta, and from the enemy's camp there came into the city the lieutenants of Mustafa and of the Agha of the Janissaries, who were met at the gate by Signor Baglione with 200 musketeers, while our officers were met by the Turks with a great array of cavalry and musketeers, accompanied by Mustafa's son in person, who welcomed them with courtesy. Signor Baglione discussed the terms of capitulation with the Turkish hostages in the city. He asked for the lives of the defenders, their arms, their goods: five cannon, three of their finest horses, and a safe passage to Candia under an escort of galleys: that the Greeks should stay in their houses and enjoy what was their own, living like Christians.

The Turks accepted these conditions, to which Mustafa assented and signed the truce. They forthwith sent galleys and sailing ships into the harbour, the soldiers began to embark, and when most of them were on board, the captains being anxious also to embark, on the morning of August 15 the right worshipful Bragadino sent me with a letter to Mustafa to say that the same evening he proposed to come out to hand to him the keys of the city, leaving the right worshipful Tiepolo in charge of the fortress. He begged that during his absence nothing should be done to annoy the citizens, for up to this time Turks and Christians had maintained with each other friendly and trustful intercourse, in all courtesy of deed and word. Mustafa replied verbally desiring me to tell the right worshipful Bragadino to come when he pleased: that he would gladly see and know him, for he recognised the great courage shown by him, his fellow officers and brave soldiers, whom, wherever he was, he should never fail to praise. On no account, let them be assured, would he suffer any annoyance to be inflicted on the citizens. I returned and reported accordingly.

In the evening, about the 21st hour, the right worshipful Bragadino, accompanied by Signor Baglione, Signor Alouigi, the illustrious Signor Gio. Anton Querini, the illustrious Signor Andrea Bragadino, Cav. dalle Haste, Cap. Carlo Ragonasco, Cap. Franc. Straco, Cap. Hettor da Brescia, Cap. Girolamo di Sacile, and other gentlemen, with 50 soldiers, went out: the officers wore their swords, the soldiers had muskets. So they went to Mustafa's tent, who at first received them courteously and made them sit down. They passed from one subject to another, then a complaint arose that during the truce Signor Bragadino had caused certain slaves to be put to death. There was not a word of truth in it, but Mustafa rising in anger would scarcely listen to what his visitors said, and ordered them to be bound. They were defenceless, for they were compelled to lay aside their arms before entering the tent, and thus bound were led one by one into the open square before the tent, and cut to pieces in Mustafa's presence.

Then twice and thrice he made Signor Bragadino, who showed no sign of fear, stretch out his neck as though he would strike off his head, but spared his life and cut off his ears and nose, and as he lay on the ground Mustafa reviled him, cursing our Saviour and saying "where now is thy Christ that He doth not help thee?" The general made never an answer. Count Hercole, one of the hostages, was also bound, but was hidden by one of Mustafa's eunuchs until his chief's fury was passed. He spared his life and made him his slave. There were three Greeks in the tent who were released, but the soldiers present in the Turkish camp were hewed in pieces, with 300 other Christians, who never dreamed of such gross perfidy and savagery. The Christians who were already embarked were thrown into chains and robbed.

The second day after the murders, August 17, Mustafa first entered the city. He caused the most worshipful Tiepolo to be hanged. I, who was in the city when the rest were slaughtered and enslaved, lay hid in Greek houses five days; but when I got no more shelter, the penalties were too great, I surrendered as a slave to a Sanjaq of Bir, with whom I stayed in the camp, my ransom being fixed at 500 sequins.

On August 17, being a Friday and their holiday, Signor Bragadino was led, Mustafa being present throughout, to the batteries built against the city and was made to carry one basket full of earth up, and another down, on each fort, and made to kiss the ground when he passed before Mustafa. Then he was led to the shore, set in a slung seat, and hoisted on the yard of a galley hung "like a stork" in view of all the slaves and Christian soldiers in the port. He was then led to the square, stripped, made to sit on the grating of the pillory, and brutally flayed alive. He bore all this with great firmness and faith, never losing heart but ever with the sternest constancy reproaching them for their broken faith. With never a sign of wavering he commended himself to God, and gave back his spirit to his Maker.

His skin was taken and stuffed with straw, and hung on the yard of a galliot, was paraded along the coast of Syria.

COUNT NESTOR MARTINENGO *was one of the officers who defended the fortifications of Famagusta for eleven months against the troops of the Turkish Commander-in-chief Lala Mustapha between 1570/71. Lala Mustapha had already conquered Nicosia, and the rest of Cyprus surrendered. But he needed the fall of Famagusta in order to report the total conquest of Cyprus for the Ottoman Empire to his overlord Sultan Selim II. The well-fortified town, cut off from all communication by land or sea, defended itself bravely under the leadership of Marc Antonio Bragadino. The betrayal by Mustapha – who promised the defenders safe passage but then put them to death – which is described here, remains even today one of the blackest and most tragic chapters in Cyprus' sad history. It still remains a traumatic event for the Greeks and is not unimportant in explaining their deep-seated fear of the Turks. Martinengo described all this in his report to the Doge after finally escaping.*

[...] "The nightingales won't let you sleep in Platres"   **Helen**

Platres: what is Platres? And this island: who knows it?
I have lived my life hearing unfamiliar names:
new countries, new idiocies of men
or of the gods;
my fate, which wavers
between the last sword of some Ajax

and another Salamis,
brought me here, to this shore,
The moon
rose from the sea like Aphrodite,
covered the Archer's stars, now moves to find
the Heart of Scorpio, and transforms all.
Truth, where is the truth?
I too was an archer in the war;
My fate: that of a man who missed his target.

GEORGE SEFERIS (1900–1971), a Greek Nobel Prize winner for Literature, often had contact with Cyprus during his life as a diplomat and poet. This has left traces in many of his poems. This excerpt comes from the poem "Helen". After the Trojan War many of the Greek heroes are supposed to have settled in Cyprus and founded city kingdoms. For Seferis his personal fate and that of these imaginary heroes is interwoven.

Cyprus

With what were these mountains woven together,
where were these mountains imprinted,
this sea, this sky,
how were they imprinted
that we use only them for comparison,
that we have only them for models?

COSTAS MONTIS (born 1914) is one of the earliest modern writers of Cyprus and, in the eyes of many, the most important. He has strongly influenced the younger generation of writers.

Black eyes

Come, dear girl, let's see those sweet black eyes of yours
That cast such sparks as only fire makes,
And if they break my poor sad heart, beloved,
Don't pity me: let them devour it.

If I should burn away and become a scorched log,
Plant me in your yard, place me anywhere:
Your face is such that on that spot, from day to day
It's possible I'll sprout, and be consoled.

And when I've taken root, and grown, and blossomed
And spread my branches, come and stand beneath them:
I'll shower all your beauty with my petals
For just one glance from your two sparkling eyes.

DIMITRIS LIPERTIS (1866–1937), a lyric poet who wrote in the Greek Cypriot dialect. Many of his poems have been set to music and are well-known as folk songs. This is one of the best-known.

Word of warning

This word is warning hangs on the wall in the reception room for visitors in the monastery of Stavrovouni near Larnaca, which is known to have the strictest rules of all the Greek Orthodox monasteries in Cyprus.

If you die before you die
then you don't die when you have to die.

Continued on page 97

St. Hilarion, the
largest of the three
forts on the Kyrenia
mountains, was
meant together with
Buffavento and
Kantara – to protect
the island from
acks from the north.

Overleaf: Bellapais
Abbey on the slopes
of the Kyrenia
mountains.

View of Kantara looking south. Kantara castle was built in the 10th century by the Byzantines in the face of the threat of Arab invasions.

House at the fishing harbour of Boghaz.

Previous page: a herd of goats in the Mesaoria plain.

86

The citadel known as "Othello's Tower" is part of the Venetian fortifications which encircle the old town of Famagusta. Above the entrance is a relief with the winged lion of St. Mark.

Overleaf: landscape on the north coast, east of Kyrenia.

87

Citrus fruits are one of Cyprus' traditional agricultural exports.

The orange harvest near Morphou. Orange and lemon groves surround the ⬮ of the same name.

The lemon harvest near Lapithos.

A typical coffee shop in Aghirda.

An upholsterer at work.

BG 6

Over against Tyre lies the island of Qubrus (Cyprus), said to be twelve days' journey round. It is full of populous cities, and offers the Muslims many advantages in their trade thither, by reason of the great quantities of merchandise, stuffs and goods, which are produced there. The island is in the power of whichever nation is overlord in these seas.

Commerce

MUQADDASI *(Shams al Din), an Arab writer (born 946), wrote his "Description of Syria" in Baghdad in 985. He mentions Cyprus and points out that Cyprus, as a result of her geographical location, has always fallen victim to the changes of power in the region.*

[…] But in excellence, Cyprus falls behind no one of the islands: for it is rich in wine and oil, and uses home-grown wheat. There are mines of copper in plenty. […]

The economy

STRABO, *a Greek geographer (63 B.C.–20 A.D.)*

[…] Together we called upon the Bellapaix muktar (village headman) whose house actually formed part of the Abbey and who waited for us on a balcony hung high above the smiling groves which stretch toward Kasaphani. He was a thick-set, handsome man in his late forties, slow in manner, with a deep true voice and a magnificent smile. […]

Bitter lemons

He questioned me quietly and discreetly about my intentions. He had already heard of the sale of the house. I told him what was in my mind and he smiled approvingly with calm self-possession. 'You'll find the people very quiet and kindly,' he said in his deep voice. 'And since you speak Greek you know that a little politeness goes a long way; but I must warn you, if you intend to try and work, not to sit under the Tree of Idleness. You have heard of it? its shadow incapacitates one for serious work. By tradition the inhabitants of Bellapaix are regarded as the laziest in the island. They are all landed men, coffee-drinkers and card-players. That is why they live to such ages. Nobody ever seems to die here. Ask Mr. Honey the grave-digger. Lack of clients has almost driven him into a decline…'

Still talking in this humorous, sardonic vein he led us through the thick grove of orange-trees to Dmitri's café, which stands outside the great barbican, and here in the sunlight I had a first glimpse of my villagers. Most of the young men and women were in the fields and Dmitri's clients were mostly grandfathers wearing the traditional baggy trousers and white cotton shirts. Gnarled as oak-trees, bent almost double by age and – who knows? – professional idleness, they were a splendid group, grey-bearded, shaggy-haired, gentle of voice and manner.

They gave us a polite good day in voices of varying gruffness, and it seemed to me from the number of crooks and sticks which had collected like a snowdrift in the corner of the tavern that many of them must have deserted their flocks for a mid-morning coffee. […]

[…] The full magnificence of the Abbey's position is not clear until one enters the inner cloister, through a superb gate decorated with marble coats of arms, and walks to the very edge of the high bluff on which it stands, the refectory windows framing the plain below with its flowering groves and curling palm-trees. We looked at each other, smiling. Kollis was too wise to waste words on it, realizing perhaps how impossible it would be to do justice to the whole prospect. He told me nothing about it, and I wished to know nothing; we simply walked in quiet, bemused friendship among those slender chipped traceries and tall-shanked columns, among the armorial shields of forgotten knights and the blazing orange-trees, until we came into the shadow of the great refectory with its high roofs where the swallows were building. […]

[…] To Larnaca through an extraordinary landscape reminding one of Plato's God 'geometrizing': low hills, almost perfect cones with levelled tops suggesting the Euclidean objects found in art studios. Wind erosion? But the panel of geometrical mounds seems handmade. And the valleys tapestried with fat-tailed sheep, plots of verdure, and here and there a camel-train and palm-tree. A strange mixture of flavours, the Bible, Anatolia, and Greece. […]

[…] The Mesaoria combines every extreme of beauty and ugliness; barren, sand-bedevilled, empty, and under moonlight a haunted waste; then in spring bursting with the shallow splendours of anemone and poppy, and cross-hatched with silk-soft vegetation. 'Only here you realize that things pushed to extremes become their opposites; the ugly barren Mesaoria and the verdant one are so extreme that one wonders whether the beauty or the ugliness has not the greater power.'

[…] Darkness? These things are relative. What does amaze one however is that the Turks, perhaps through lack of a definite cultural pattern of their own, or of one worth imposing on the Greeks, left them freedom of religion, language and even local government – and indeed vested in them a large part of the Imperial administration: a recognition perhaps of the enviable qualities of restlessness and imagination which they themselves lacked. When modern Greece, therefore, emerged once more into the light of day as a geographical entity in 1821, it was as a step-child of Greek Byzance. For nearly four hundred years the Orthodox Church had served as a repository for the native genius or ethos of these latter-day Byzantines. Language had been carefully preserved, so that apart from a few Turkish suffixes and a few score borrowed words Greek was still manifestly Greek, and the average Greek community emerged from the Turkish occupation less changed psychologically, say, than the British did from the Norman. Much that was Turkish in the way of manners, cookery, and so on was retained, but even this residue was soon infused with a liveliness quite foreign to the stately old-fashioned Turkish style with its contemplative and luxurious indolence. […]

Things were no different in Cyprus. […]

LAWRENCE DURRELL *(born 1912) lived in Cyprus for a few years during the fifties, first as a writer in Bellapais and later as a press officer in the British Colonial Administration in Nicosia. His book "Bitter Lemons" is one of the loveliest books about Cyprus, her people, history and landscape.*

The population of Levkosia numbers about 20,000, but the exact number of inhabitants cannot be ascertained, the women not being included in the census. The majority of the inhabitants are Turks, although they are nearly equalled in number by the Greeks. There are besides a few Armenians, about eighty to ninety Roman Catholics, and no Jews at all. [...]

[...] The language of the Turks in Cyprus is very pure; they say it is the best after that spoken at Constantinople. The Cyprian Greek, however, is more of a dialect, and contains many Italian words, as also a number of Turkish expressions. The Turkish language is that most generally used at Levkosia; we found very few men who could not speak that language, and a great many who knew Turkish only; even most of the Greek women are perfectly acquainted with it. A very widely-spread usage may be mentioned here, according to which Greeks or Turks will never say 'no', but simply lift up their heads, without uttering a word, as a sign of negation. [...]

[...] Visitors always receive jam made of melons, cherries, quince, apricots, the juice of the crataegus plant, or rose-leaves. With this sweet-stuff, called Tatli in Turkish, Glikon in Greek, the servants bring little baskets of silverware with small ornamental spoons: these are divided into two compartments, one for the clean spoons, the other for those which have been used. After that comes the coffee, as a sort of invitation to leave, especially with the Turks. If the visitor bores his host, a second cup of coffee will soon follow: if he is liked, he is on the contrary kept waiting a long while for his coffee. After the coffee, cigarettes are usually offered, and a servant brings small brass plates for the ashes. It is a peculiar custom with the Greeks, and is considered a sign of exceptional politeness, to put a chair before the feet of the visitor, who places them on the lower bar, and he is not obliged then to keep his feet on the cold marble floor. The Turks keep their Sabbath in Cyprus not on Friday, but with the Greeks on Sunday, on which day the streets are most quiet, and the Bazaars, which are open in the morning only, look as still and solitary as graveyards. All the offices are closed on Sundays. [...]

[...] Weddings and circumcisions are celebrated with great festivities by the Turks, both by men and women. The men occupy the first rank. In the bride's room a blind man plays the

The Cypriot life-style

violin. The wedding ceremonies begin invariably on Mondays and terminate on Thursday night. The women first goes to the bath. An Imam (priest) enters a dark room in which the bride and bridegroom are, says a prayer, and leaves them alone then. The marriage contract is made in presence of witnesses, the woman appearing veiled. The man has to deposit a certain sum of money, which becomes the property of his wife in case he deserts her. After this, the woman and her dresses and other things belonging to her outfit are promenaded through the streets with great pomp. […]

[…] At Greek weddings (Greeks cannot marry any nearer relative than their third cousins) the priest walks three times round a table, and then throws cotton-seeds and coins into the air, which are given by the male witnesses: the two female witnesses have to pay for the bride's wreath. The next day all of them pay a visit to the newly-married couple, bringing presents to the bride, who also receives many presents from the parents and relations. […]

ARCHDUKE LUDWIG SALVATOR OF AUSTRIA *visited Nicosia in 1873 during his extensive travels. His book "Nicosia, the capital of Cyprus" was first published anonymously in German in Prague in 1873 and later in English in London in 1881.*

The difference between Greeks and Turks

The difference between Greek and Turk, said Kemal, stemmed from his people belonging to a vaster and older land. 'Listen. I will tell you the respective qualities of ourselves and the Greeks. These are simple, obvious.' He left a moment's silence to emphasize the importance of his thoughts. Below, the masts of ships, lit up in the harbour, were moving and winking over the crenellations; above us the shell of St. George of the Greeks reared on the stars.

'First,' said Kemal, 'while the Greeks are fun-loving, the Turks are terrible' – by the *terribilita* he meant something awesome and formidable – 'and where the Greeks are materialists and lovers of luxury, we are simple and moral.'

In a sense I could agree with this, but it was clear to what conclusions his arguments were tending, and already a ghostly dissenting Greek had arisen in my mind.

'This austerity explains why we live as we do.' He pointed to some poor houses nearby. 'Now the Greeks mistake that for poverty. But I myself live in a house no larger in Nicosia, and I've never wanted for anything. And I'm a typical Turk. Yes...' He relished the thought with a romanticism which betrayed its falseness. 'I am the Turk-in-the-street.'

I mumbled: 'You're not typical.'

'I am,' he repeated. 'And why not? Let the ant keep to its size. I represent my people.'

'I've found your people vary.'

He ignored this, but buttonholed me with his gaze. 'Now the Greeks are crafty. They prostitute themselves...' *Adaptable and intelligent,* answered the ghostly Greek in me. '... While the Turks are more solemn.' Stupid, said the soundless voice, growing bigoted.

'Simplicity, morality, dignity.' Kemal clasped his big hands together. 'So you see, the first Greek characteristic is Slave! The first Turkish one is Ruler!'

But the simple, the moral and the dignified, whispered my phantom Greek, no longer rule.

[…] Next morning I walked round the city walls, tramping along the dry fosse cut in its solid rock. A few palm trees leant dusty and small against the fifty-foot ramparts. Within the city the earth sloped up to the parapets in grass-covered mounds. Only at the embrasures did the thickness of the defences become apparent, where the line of bastions, with stubbled walls and sonorous names, dropped sheer to the moat and its dwarfish trees.

Their loneliness filled my mind with the siege. I sat down by the crenellated scarp, unnerved by their memorial solitude. […]

COLIN THUBRON, *an Englishman, hiked more than a thousand kilometres through Cyprus in 1971. His impressions of the island and its people were published in his book "Journey into Cyprus". The excerpt here records a conversation with Kemal, a Turkish Cypriot.*

Growing up in Cyprus

May 19 is one of the corner stones in Turkish history. In 1919 Atatürk came ashore at Samsun and that was the beginning of the New Turkey. This day in Nicosia was celebrated every year, on public platforms, nationalist speeches, poems were declaimed, school children from several schools were to be seen waving small Turkish flags to the tune of military marches. In Minareli Köy, however, things went more quietly. After a small speech from father on the great importance of the day, the bright children of the class would read poems. Just like at the end of Ramazan I would be dressed in my very best clothes.

It was a gloriously sunny day, we were sweating in our shirt sleeves. Either the muhtar or some other such personage had come to our school to hear us. Blood and words ran high. Anti-Greek sentiment too. How the Turks had fought to get rid of the Megalo Idea.

We were about to disperse, the afternoon classes were unofficially called off, when Ozkul and some other boys from his grade asked us to return to school after lunch. The secret tone, the secret intention.

When we met at the back of our school, all boys, Ozkul stood on the steps of the entrance and said something like: Today we must take revenge on those who killed our brothers on the Turkish soil. We shouted our consent. Then we were platooned neatly, one sixther heading each juvenile group and dispersed in the fields, keeping contact with our groups through coded whistles.

We made our way, through the southern outskirts of the village, into the Greek occupied territory. At that time of the day lots of children were bound to be in the fields, parents being either in the village for lunch and siesta or something else. Everything went according to our strategy. We met a group of Greek children playing lazily, the sun was hot, the corn was bravely erect and turning yellow. We crawled on elbows and knees through the corn and waited for the signal from Ozkul. He whistled piercingly. We jumped up and shouted: Samsun, Samsun, all the Greeks out, out! The Greek boys left their sticks, shocked, amazed. They saw us, about ten of us, they were at the most four or five. The Turks, the Turks, they shouted and began to run through

102

the fields. Ozkul yelled, brandishing his long stick as if it were a zataghan (sword). We upset their 'stove' and ran after them. Only one little boy couldn't run fast enough and collapsed on the ground, panting and crying his eyes out. We stood round him, giggling, triumphant. He looked like a beetle lying there, covering his head with both arms. No one wanted to take any action. Ozkul wasn't at all pleased. He was planning to capture older boys. One little boy! But he said to us, if we take him with us the others will go and fetch help from Trahon and then we'll have a real battle. We pricked the boy to get up and he got up and I realised this was Andrikko, the son of the owner of the coffee house behind our house. His eyes turned to me and I said to Ozkul: No, this is the son of my father's friend. Ozkul said: No friends in this battle. We must get rid of the Greeks otherwise they'll want to strangle us one day. Andrikko looked at me again not knowing what we were talking about. He didn't speak a word of Turkish. I said to him in my limited Greek vocabulary: Don't be afraid, my friend! His eyes smiled. Ozkul said to me: There is no reason to talk to him. Back to your groups. Quick, quick!

We kept poor little Andrikko ahead of us his hand raised up. Our sticks pointing towards him. He sobbed as he marched on. We took him to a little hut in a field. Ozkul, Osman and myself remained in the hut with Andrikko. The other children took position round the hut and one boy went further as an emissary. We were quite sure the escaped Greek boys would muster force and come back in search of our prisoner.

Ozkul was exercising some form of cruelty on Andrikko. Such as keeping his head under his own arms. At one point he said Andrikko should take off his trousers and we should beat his bottom and then make him bend down against the sun. Andrikko instinctively understood what was coming and tried to escape. This caused him a nose bleed from Osman's elbow and he sat sobbing in one corner of the hut.

The emissary rushed to the hut followed by the defenders. He was afraid and could hardly speak. Ozkul said: Tell us, then. Who's coming? The little boy from the second form said loudly: Our fathers. The shock of this information was indescribable. No sooner we heard what he had said than we left our prisoner to his misery and dashed to the village.

Then I heard father's voice: he was calling my name. The growl of an angry lion. I became smaller and smaller.

I received several sharp slaps from him. I was entirely molten, I trickled on the verandah, another slap and I would be gone.

This is the last thing I expected from our son, father was saying. How am I going to live down this monstrous behaviour? Do you think I'm going to let this kind of barbarism continue? When I do everything to teach them good manners, brotherhood and all the necessary qualities a civilised person requires? Oh, no. Another slap. Mother said: Enough, darling, enough!

If I only knew that the other boys were being punished in the same way just now! Father said: If they are not, they will be, tomorrow. I'll teach them what it is to take the entire history into their own hands. I had never seen him so sincerely upset and although I hated each slap I received, I harboured no resentment. Especially as I knew Andrikko.

Andrikko came with his father later that evening after my parents had had their dinner. I was given nothing to eat. I saw Andrikko holding his father's hand in the courtyard. The hurricane lamp was somewhere there as usual. After a few words from both fathers I was allowed to go out and embrace Andrikko. Then his father took me to the coffee house and gave me a cool drink of aniseed, sweet and embracing.

TANER BAYBARS, *a Turkish Cypriot writer born in 1937 in a village on the north coast of Cyprus, lives today, like so many of his compatriots, in London. In his sensitive book "Plucked in a Far-off Land" he describes the carefree years of his childhood before Cyprus – still under colonial rule – was torn by communal strife, and the two communities lived together often in mixed villages. The book is particularly important because it is written by a Turkish Cypriot. In the above, slightly abridged, scene he describes how a group of Turkish schoolboys in a mixed village decide "to show the Greeks" on the Turkish national day, 19th May. Taner's father is a school-teacher and also teaches his son's class.*

Overleaf: vine cultivation in the hinterland of Paphos, near Polis.

Travel Guide

Historical summary

In the *early history* of the Eastern Mediterranean (6000–2500 B.C.) Cyprus was inhabited, probably as early as 6000 B.C., by people whose origin is unknown. They were probably settlers from Asia Minor who moved to the island. The most important of the early Stone Age settlements are Khirokitia, Sotira, Erimi, Petra tou Limnitis and Kalavassos (named after their respective sites). During this period an agricultural village culture was dominant.

Cyprus became interesting to its neighbours during *the Copper Age* (around 2500 B.C.). The rich copper deposits probably gave the island its name (Kypros in Greek). However, it may even go back to the Hebrew word "Kopher" meaning "healing plant", and Cyprus may then have passed on its name to the coveted metal (aes caprium in Latin, which means Cypriot ore). The island traded with the outside world, especially with the Near East (Phoenicia and Egypt) but also with Crete.

During the *Bronze Age* (2500–1050 B.C.) Cyprus became a cultural centre. The focal point of the island was Alasia (Engomi/Famagusta) founded around 1900 B.C.

The production of bronze weapons and work implements developed after the introduction of techniques from the Near East.

The art of pottery-making blossomed, influenced by the Egyptians and Minoan Crete. The conflict between the Hittites and the Egyptians for domination of this area affected Cyprus, which had relations with both powers and finally became a vassal-state of the Egyptians, who called it "Asi, rich in copper".

Around the middle of the 2nd millenium B.C., Achaean Greeks from the mainland reached the island and settled there. Their Mycenaen culture took hold in Cyprus. This is probably the most important period in Cyprus' past. This Hellenic colonialisation has formed and dominated the island for more than three thousand years, up to the present day. Around 1200 B.C. a second wave of Greek settlers reached the island, this time probably in some way connected with the Trojan War. After the end of the war many of the Greek heroes stopped off in Cyprus on their way back to their homeland. They founded many cities and city states on the island, including Salamis, Kourion, Ledra, Amathus, Kition, and Soli. The Greek language and hellenic culture dominated in Cyprus.

During the *Iron Age* (1050–475 B.C.) Cyprus fell victim to the struggle for power between the Egyptians and the Assyrians. The latter called it "the land of the setting sun". The Cypriot city-kingdoms supported the Assyrians and after their defeat by the Babylonians, Cyprus once again came under Egyptian influence. At the same time the Phoenicians increased their commercial activity in Cyprus. Larnaca, known as Kition to the Greeks, was founded by the Phoenicians.

Around 700 B.C. the Assyrians again became the most important power in the Near East, and the kings of Cyprus became vassals to the Assyrians.

The Assyrians were followed by the Egyptians and finally the Persians. The kings of Cyprus revolted against the domination of the Persians, but without success. Nevertheless the citystates developed into booming commercial and cultural centres.

Cyprus then fell under the *rule of the Ptolemies* (325–58 B.C.) after the island supported Alexander the Great against the Persians.

The power of the city-kingdoms ended with Nicocreon of Salamis and Pygmalion of Kition. Lefkosia, which later became Nicosia, and Paphos took over from Salamis as the most important centre in the island. The rule of the Ptolemies, which was a rich period culturally, came to an end around 58 B.C.

Roman times. The Romans then ruled for more than four hundred years until 390 A.D. Cyprus became the first country to be ruled by a Christian following the conversion of the Proconsul Sergius Paulus in Paphos by the Apostle Paul. It experienced centuries of prosperity. At the beginning of the Christian era the island had more than a million inhabitants, while Salamis alone had 200,000.

When the Roman Empire was divided up in 390 A.D., Cyprus came under *Byzantine rule*, which then lasted till 1191 A.D. This was the longest-lasting epoch which the island experienced, although it was also interrupted by frequent Arab invasions. Byzantium with its Greco-Christian culture has remained till today the most important cultural influence in Cyprus.

After a short interlude in 1191, when the English King *Richard the Lionheart* took Cyprus from the last "emperor" of Cyprus, Isaac Komnenos, during the Third Crusade, the island was sold for 100,000 gold dinars to the *Knights Templar* the following year. The Knights Templar, fearing a revolt of the Greek population against them, gave it back to Richard the Lionheart. But in 1192 the island was given to the French Crusader Guy de Lusignan, who was at the time "King of Jerusalem".

The period of *Catholic Lusignan* rule which lasted till 1489, a full three hundred years, was one of peace and prosperity. Impressive monuments such as the Gothic cathedrals of Nicosia and Famagusta and the Abbey of Bellapais still bear witness to this. The population, nevertheless, experienced this period with mixed feelings. The Roman Church suppressed the Orthodox Church, even persecuted it. But the Greek population remained faithful to its beliefs. On the whole, however, these three hundred years were definitive for a first far-reaching Europeanisation of Cyprus.

The period of Venetian rule. Genoa and Venice competed with one another for Cyprus while the Lusignans still ruled. The last Queen of Cyprus, Caterina Cornaro, abdicated in 1489. After that, for almost a hundred years the Venetian banners fluttered over the island. These years were also prosperous years for Cyprus which had commercial contacts with all parts of the known world of that time. The Venetians strengthened the city fortifications of Nicosia, Kyrenia and Famagusta during the last years of their rule in view of the growing danger from the Turks.

Turkish rule. In 1570/71 the Ottoman Turks under Sultan Selim II, represented by his Commander-in-chief Lala Mustapha, conquered Cyprus. The betrayal by Lala Mustapha of the heroic defender of Famagusta, Marc Antonio Bragadino, is even today a traumatic event which every Cypriot can picture in his mind's eye.

At first, however, the Greek population greeted the Islamic Turks as liberators after four hundred years of religious and intellectual repression by the Latin Roman Church. However, under the Ottomans the island quickly became a thinly populated and impoverished province on the outskirts of this gigantic empire.

At the beginning of their rule the Turks converted the Catholic cathedrals into mosques. Almost all Greek churches were allowed to function as such. The Archbishop of Cyprus, the head of the Orthodox Church of Cyprus, was recognised by the Sultan as the Ethnarch, that is to say the political leader as well as the spiritual leader of the Greek population. For a time the Archbishop had as much power as the Turkish Governor, to whom he paid over the taxes which he collected from the Greek population.

With the Turks came settlers from Anatolia to the island, the forefathers of the present-day Turkish Cypriots. They established themselves as farmers and craftsmen, while commerce and money-lending remained in the hands of the Greeks.

After the start of the Greek War of Independence in 1821, the relationship between the Greeks and Turks in Cyprus became more strained. The Governor had the whole of the Greek elite slaughtered in a cruel and bloody massacre in 1821. The desire of the Greeks for "Enosis", the union of the island with Greece, stems from this time.

The British administration. In 1878 Cyprus came under the control of the British. The British wanted a bastion to secure their land and sea routes to their eastern colonies, above all India. They reorganised the administrative and educational systems of Cyprus and the island experienced a second, this time decisive, phase of Europeanisation. The legal system was based on the British model and the whole infrastructure was improved.

At the outbreak of the First World War, Britain offered Greece union with Cyprus on condition that Greece would fight on Britain's side. Greece refused, Cyprus was then annexed and became a British Crown Colony in 1925.

In 1955 the Greek Cypriot underground movement EOKA, supported by the Orthodox Church, began its fight against British domination, and Archbishop Makarios defended the bloody struggle in the face of world public opinion. The military leader of EOKA was Georgios Grivas, a Cypriot-born retired Greek army officer. The aim of Grivas and Makarios was not only to free the island from colonial domination but to unite it with Greece, "Enosis". This became emphatically clear to the Turkish population, which therefore became the natural ally of the British in this bloody confrontation. And this in turn brought upon them the wrath of EOKA.

There were many conflicts between the Greeks and the Turks. And the two communities, which had up till then by and large lived peacefully and often in mixed villages with one another, became more and more estranged.

In 1958/59, Britain, Greece and Turkey held discussions in Zurich and London over the fate of the island. They ended with a compromise – there would be no Enosis, which was the goal of eighty per cent of the population of the island, but there would also be no partition of the island, as favoured by the Turkish twenty per cent of the population. Instead Cyprus would become an independent state. Britain, Greece and Turkey would act together as guarantor powers and watch over the implementation of the new constitution.

In 1960 Cyprus was given *independence.* Great Britain retained two sovereign military bases on the island, Akrotiri and Dhekelia. Under the constitution the Turks got more than their proportional rights. Although they were only twenty per cent of the population, they got thirty per cent representation in the administration and forty per cent representation in the police and army. This led to conflict although Makarios, as the new President of Cyprus, had signed the London agreement, that is to say, the constitution.

A further problem for the young Republic was the economic imbalance between Greeks and Turks. At the end of 1963 trouble broke out after Makarios told the Turkish Vice-President, Dr. Kütchük, that he wanted to amend the constitution, which was not functioning in certain areas. Greek extremists who still dreamed of Enosis then attacked the smaller Turkish community.

As a consequence of this civil strife the United Nations intervened. In some areas of Cyprus the Turks cut themselves off in enclaves from which they inexorably expelled the Greeks, just as the EOKA fanatics spread fear and terror amongst the island's Turks and forced them out of home and village. The unitary state collapsed in a few weeks.

The administration, which is now in the hands of the Greeks, remains internationally recognised till today. The talks between the two communities on a new constitution and a new start together dragged on for years, and in 1973 were on the brink of a breakthrough. But it never came about.

In July 1974 the military coup against Makarios, carried out by the National Guard instigated by the Athens military regime, brought the former EOKA fighter Nicos Sampson to power. Makarios survived but had to flee from the island. A week later Turkey answered the coup, which had led to the breakdown of the constitution of Cyprus, with an invasion of the island in order to protect the safety of the Turkish Cypriots, since within the Greek community the supporters and opponents of Makarios were engaged in bloody conflict. Turkey came up against hard military resistance from the Greek Cypriots, but within three days managed to build a bridgehead near Kyrenia in the north and to join up with the Turkish enclave in the north of Nicosia.

During a four-week ceasefire – which was in fact not respected – Great Britain, Greece (whose military regime fell after the coup in Cyprus), Turkey and the Cypriot Government held discussions in Geneva. In Cyprus the President of the Parliament Clerides took over from Sampson as Acting President in accordance with the constitution. The Greek side found it impossible to accept the situation resulting from the military invasion, particularly since Turkey continually set new ultimatums.

In mid-August the Turkish invasion forces, about 40,000 soldiers with massive air and sea support and 300 tanks, broke out of the corridor between Nicosia and Kyrenia to the west and east. Within three days the island was divided by the Turkish army. About 200,000 Greek Cypriots fled or were expelled from the north.

The Turkish army conquered about thirty-eight per cent of the territory of the Republic of Cyprus, in which about seventy per cent of the national resources were to be found. In the following months Turkish Cypriots living in the south of the island were resettled in the north, they too became victims of the long-smouldering Cyprus conflict.

In February 1975 the Turkish Cypriot leader Denktash declared the north to be the "Turkish Federated State of Cyprus". His goal is to re-organise Cyprus into a bi-zonal federation with a Turkish area in the north and a Greek area in the south. This was agreed by him in principle with President Makarios who returned to his offices of Archbishop and President in December 1974. However, Makarios died suddenly in August 1977. His successor Kyprianou – who has been ruling in alliance with the strong pro-Moscow Communist Party AKEL since 1983 – has

108

Continued on page 117

*A chapel on the
north coast, east
of Kyrenia.*

The Monastery of Stavrovouni, built on the top of a mountain near Larnaca, has been an important place of pilgrimage since it was founded in 327 B.C.

110

The Byzantine Church of Yero-skipos, dating from the 11th century, and the Church of St. Hilarion and St. Barnabas in Peristerona (below) are both typical examples of Cypriot style churches with five domes.

Overleaf: Pano Lefkara.

111

On the foothills
of the Troodos
mountains near
Paphos.

Previous page:
landscape west of
Kyrenia, near Orga

not been able to get the Cyprus problem out of the deadlock. The Turkish side insists on a fifty-fifty division of all important posts and institutions, a weak central government and two federal bodies with far-reaching competence. Since 1974, all efforts to bring the two sides nearer have failed.

The declaration of the north as an independent state, "The Turkish Republic of Northern Cyprus" in November 1983 has made the possibility of a joint solution even more remote. This creation is considered illegal by the Greek side and by the United Nations. Apart from Turkey, which in fact controls it, it is not recognised by any other state. The partition of Cyprus is likely to last a long time.

Useful information

Cyprus is the third largest island in the Mediterranean and has an area of 9251 square kilometres. It is about 230 kilometres from west to east and just over 100 kilometres from north to south. The coastline is 780 kilometres long. The island lies 70 kilometres as the crow flies from the south coast of Turkey and 90 kilometres from Syria, but about 850 kilometres from the Greek capital, Athens.

Population

Cyprus has today about 680,000 inhabitants. Of these about 510,000 live in the south and 170,000 in the north of the island. Included in the figure of 170,000 are about 35,000 new settlers who have been brought over from the Anatolian mainland to the Turkish controlled area. They are not Turkish Cypriots in the historical sense, neither were they born on the island nor can they trace their origins back to the Ottoman Empire. The following figures give one a general picture: eighty per cent of Cypriots are of Greek, and 20 per cent of Turkish origin. About thirty-eight per cent of the territory of the Republic of Cyprus, the northern part, has been controlled by Turkey since 1974.

The state

The Republic of Cyprus, which has been an independent state since 1960, is a member of the British Commonwealth and the United Nations. It has an association with the EEC but, unlike Greece and Turkey, is not a member of NATO.

At this point it is worth noting that the internationally recognised government of Cyprus which rules on the Greek side in the south does not recognise the north. It has therefore a specific legal interpretation and practice which it has applied in this connection since the occupation and partition in 1974. Travellers who enter the country from the north, that is to say via Turkey, are considered illegal and in contravention of the law. As a result anyone who enters the island from the occupied north cannot visit the south of the island but will be turned back at the only checkpoint near the former Ledra Palace Hotel and may possibly even be prosecuted.

Greece has also followed suit, and when one has a stamp from northern Cyprus in one's passport, one is not able to enter Greece either. The Turkish authorities behave in a similar manner; however, they are more flexible where tourists are concerned. It is possible to get permission to spend a day in the northern part of Nicosia, Famagusta (only the old town), and Kyrenia and Bellapais Abbey. In order to get the pass, one has to request it in person and enter the Turkish side via the Ledra Palace Hotel checkpoint. The pass is usually available twenty-four hours later, and it is only possible to get it on the same day in exceptional cases on presentation of one's passport. This means that one has to make the trip twice. The issuing officers for these passes do not work at weekends.

In planning a trip, therefore, one should take into account that one can enter the north from the south when one only stays a day, but that one cannot enter the south from the north. The availability of these passes varies depending on the current political situation and often changes without notice. As a matter of principle, the Government of Cyprus only recognises entry into the island via the airports of Larnaca and Paphos, or via the ports of Limassol, Larnaca and Paphos.

Ways of reaching Cyprus

Numerous airlines fly into Larnaca, including Lufthansa, Cyprus Airways, Austrian Airlines, Swissair, Sabena, KLM and British Airways. In addition there are favourable charter flights to Larnaca and more recently to Paphos.

It is also possible to reach Cyprus via the East Berlin airport Schönefeld and in addition to East German airlines, the national airlines of Czechoslovakia, Hungary, Rumania and Bulgaria also fly into Larnaca, as do many airlines from the Near East. Ercan airport in the north of the island can only be reached via Istanbul and is not used by any international airline other than Turkish Airlines.

There are regular car ferry services from Greece which generally start from Piraeus and travel via Rhodes to Cyprus and then on to Syria, Lebanon or Israel. There are also ferry services from various Italian ports.

The flight from Frankfurt or Cologne/Bonn is about four hours. The sea voyage from Piraeus takes about forty-eight hours, depending on the boat.

Travel formalities

Citizens of the Federal Republic of Germany, Switzerland or Austria need a passport which has a validity of at least three months. An identity card is not sufficient. A visa is not required for a stay of up to three months, but may be asked for by the relevant authority in Nicosia in cases of a longer stay.

Car

Anyone who wants to bring their own car to Cyprus does not require a Carnet de Passage, the German documents are sufficient (road licence and driving licence). The international green insurance card, however, is not valid in Cyprus. One should therefore take out insurance for the period of stay on entry into the ports of Limassol or Larnaca. No tax or custom duties are payable on the car for a period of up to three months. An extension (which should be applied for in good time) up to six months is possible, and in exceptional cases even up to a year.

Car insurance taken out for Cyprus is not valid when the car is taken into the north.

There are representatives of all the large European car manufacturers who can supply a good selection of the usual spare parts. So it is not necessary to take half the garage along with you, as is perhaps advisable when travelling in some other countries in the region. However, spare parts are often expensive in view of the high customs duties. Wages on the other hand are still lower than in Europe. As the cost of ferries from Piraeus is high, it is only worth taking a car if one intends to stay in Cyprus for some time.

Rented cars

It is possible to hire a car anywhere in the island at reasonable rates, even for longer stays. Although the exceptionally cheap rates which were available a few years ago have risen drastically due to the growing

You can book a seat for a particular time in advance, for instance over the telephone from your hotel, and you will be collected punctually. Or you can go to the taxi office departure points (most are near to each other) and can take the next departing taxi. Prices are fixed and low. It is not possible to bargain and even less to be cheated.

If one hires a taxi in town or between towns then the driver must use the meter which has now been installed in all taxis on the island. However, in the case of long trips one can settle the price in advance. Usually the price is much lower if one takes the same taxi for the return trip.

Currency

The local currency is the Cyprus pound; at the moment the exchange rate is about DM 4.90. The old division into 1000 mils which dated from colonial times was phased out at the end of 1983 in favour of the more internationally up-to-date 100 cents. There are C£10, C£5, C£1 and 50 cent notes, and coins of 20, 10, 5, 2, 1 and 1/2 cent. One is only allowed to take C£10 in Cypriot currency into and out of the country. Foreign currency may be brought into the country without limit, but it is best to declare amounts in cash of over 500 dollars when one enters the country so that one can take them out again without any problems. Traveller's cheques and Eurocheques are accepted by all banks – of which there are many – and also by most hotels. The same goes naturally for all the important European currencies. Eurocheques are, however, not accepted by shops.

The same applies to the north, where the Turkish lira has been introduced since partition in 1974. However, one can pay in Cyprus pounds, which are accepted by all gladly since they can be used to pay for goods on the black market which are not available or are in short supply in the north. However, one must pay the authorities and for entry into museums in Turkish lira. In the south, though, this currency is useless and no-one will accept it.

tourism, prices are still much lower than in Europe. An Opel Kadett or a Mazda, for example, costs about C£ 10–13 per day, including full insurance cover. There is no extra charge per mile and no limit on the mileage. Many international car hire firms are represented in Cyprus but there are also many smaller local firms. As the prices vary and as it is possible to bargain (as with many other services and purchases) especially in the case of long-term arrangements, one should compare prices before one decides. In the tourist centres it is also possible to hire bicycles and mopeds as well as cars. By now also package tours – including car and hotel vouchers – are offered by European travel agencies. In this way one can enjoy the conveniances of an organized journey combined with individual freedom.

Road travel

The roads between the main towns are in fairly good condition though usually narrower than similar roads in Europe. Side roads are usually eaten away at the edges, if they are asphalted at all; there is usually only room for one car on the narrow band of asphalt. Overtaking and passing are therefore more risky since one of the two drivers has to move off the road. In the case of two passing cars this tends to become a battle of nerves: who is going to move off the road? Usually both make way for each other at the very last moment.

In Cyprus one drives on the left. The discipline of the local drivers, particularly of the service taxis, gets worse from year to year. So it is best to be careful. The winding country roads are dangerous, especially since Cypriots love to overtake on bends and steep inclines with no visibility. Even in the big towns the discipline of former colonial times has now been forgotten. Generally cars move so far into the crossing that pedestrians have no chance to cross the street in peace and cars turning right or left give pedestrians no chance at all. In general it is easier to get used to the local drivers than in Greece or Turkey, and one drives here at no more risk. Since hired cars have special red number plates, one can count on the local drivers to show more care and understanding.

Transportation

is excellent. Buses travel regularly between all main towns and villages. Often they are old buses from British colonial times with a high chassis to take account of the bad roads. In addition there are service taxis, which means that the fare is divided among all the passengers. They travel regularly between all towns in the north as well as in the south.

Shops, opening times

Working hours are strictly adhered to. Usually local authorities and banks are only open in the morning from 8 a.m. to 1 p.m., shops are also open in the afternoons from 3 to 6 p.m. Everything is closed on Saturday afternoon and all day Sunday – with British consistency. The only exceptions are a few cafés and flower shops. Petrol stations are also closed at weekends, although there is always one open for emergencies.

In winter time, working hours are slightly different. Many shops remain open during midday and therefore close earlier in the afternoon. Museums and archaeological sites are open from 8 a.m. to 2 p.m., some also in the afternoons. In some places there is a midday break. In winter, opening hours are usually shorter, so it is advisable to check in advance before visiting sites. In general museums are closed on Sundays and holidays, while open-air excavation sites are usually open for some hours. As far as the island's churches are concerned, which are often of great artistic and historical interest, the village priest or monk usually has the key and often one has to search for him. The most likely place to find him is at home or in his favourite coffee shop. A small donation for the church is much appreciated.

In the monasteries, decent clothing is a must although the strict monks have become a bit more liberal of late. Often it depends on the monk who is on duty at the time. Ladies should not enter the church in shorts and should cover their shoulders even in the height of summer. Usually there is a notice at the entrance to the monastery calling attention to this.

Since 1983 women are no longer allowed to enter Stavrovouni monastery near Larnaca, and have to wait behind a fence until the male visitors or family members return from the visit. Exceptions are only made on Sundays.

Medical treatment

Medical treatment in Cyprus is in general good. There are hospitals in all towns, although they do not come up to European standards.

Medical training is of a high standard. Most doctors have studied in England, and the younger ones on the Greek side have often studied in the Federal Republic of Germany or the German Democratic Republic; on the Turkish side, in Turkey. Since nearly all doctors speak English, there are hardly any problems of communication. In addition to the hospitals there are many private clinics which are usually to be preferred.

Pharmacies are to be found practically on every corner, all medicines are available, often imported from England or Greece. There are also many German products available which often cost only about a quarter of what they cost in Germany.

In the Turkish north, one may have problems getting specific medicines due to lack of foreign exchange. In general however medical attention is up to standard, if more modest than in the south.

Travel seasons and clothing

In general Cyprus offers ideal travel conditions all the year round. The pleasantest months are March till mid-May and then October and November. At these times of the year the temperatures are similar to Europe in summer (18°–25°C). In the evenings, however, it is considerably cooler, especially in the mountains but even in Nicosia. From the middle of May until the beginning of October it is hot. The average temperatures on the coast are 32°C and in the interior of the island 40°C. There is very little rain in summer. The winter rains, from the end of October till April, usually only last for an hour or so here and there over the island and then make way again for blue skies. The heavy rains which go on for hours in Europe are very rare in Cyprus.

In February, snowfalls on the Troodos mountains offer the possibility of skiing. This is one of the main attractions of the island for tourists from Arab countries – most of them have never seen snow before in their life. On weekends one meets the whole of Nicosia on the white slopes of Mount Olympus.

Water temperatures after the middle of May are pleasant for bathing at around 21°C. It is possible to bathe until mid-December. Clothing should be adjusted according to the season. A warm pullover is always necessary, and in winter a coat as well. There is a considerable drop in temperature between day and night. For hiking in the Troodos mountains, which is growing in popularity, solid walking shoes are a must.

Accommodation

In the south there are more than 100 hotels with about 12,000 beds. The majority are first class or luxury hotels. Smaller hotels with family management and pensions are rare. In addition, however, it is possible to make private arrangements.

Basically it is possible to find something for every taste and pocketbook. Prices have risen greatly in recent years. Cyprus is no longer the cheap tourist resort that it once was. Nevertheless prices are reasonable for what one gets. The standard of the hotels, the service and the meals are notably better than in Greece or Turkey.

Hotel prices are fixed by the government and must be displayed in rooms. Prices in restaurants and taverns are also controlled by the state.

In the north, formerly Greek-owned hotels are now run by Turkish Cypriots and the Greek side considers this unlawful (hence the strict controls when one returns from a day trip to the north). There is almost no foreign tourism in the north, other than from Turkey, nevertheless prices are not low.

There are *youth hostels* in Nicosia, Larnaca, Limassol and Paphos. During the holiday season they are hopelessly full, as is other reasonable accommodation, so it is advisable to book in advance.

Camping

Camping is possible but at the moment is still in its infancy. In the south there are official camping sites in Troodos, Pyla near Larnaca, and in Polis. In addition one can sometimes camp on private ground, provided one obtains permission in advance.

Telephone, post

The telephone code for Cyprus from Germany is 00357. From Cyprus one can dial directly to all European countries. The code for the Federal Republic of Germany is 0049, for Switzerland 0041, for Great Britain 0044.

Airmail takes about one week to reach Germany, postcards in the holiday season may take up to three weeks.

Customs

All personal effects can be taken in and out of the country without any problem. Alcoholic drinks and cigarettes in the usual quantities, technical and optical instruments only in such quantities as are necessary for personal use. The importation of narcotics, weapons and walkie-talkies is strictly forbidden and controls are stringent.

It is only possible to take antiquities out of the country if one has permission from the relevant suthorities (Ministry of Interior, Department of Antiquities). Such permission is only given in special cases or when the object in question has no special historical or artistic value. Illegal export of antiques is subject to prosecution. It is best to be careful when antiques are offered for sale in the north, since this is considered illegal by the Greek side and in addition many are fakes.

Diplomatic representation

Embassy of the U.S.A., Dositheos and Therissos Street, Nicosia. Tel. 46 51 51.

British High Commission, Alex Pallis Street, Nicosia. Tel. 47 31 31.

Australia High Commission, 4 Annis Komnenis Street, Nicosia. Tel. 47 30 01.

Consulate of Canada, Themistocles Dervis Street, Nicosia, Julia House. Tel. 45 16 30.

Places of interest

Note: after the partition of the island many of the usual place names in the north have been changed. All towns and villages have been given Turkish names. Many were in any case previously used by the Turks, e.g. Magoşa for the old town of Famagusta or Girne for Kyrenia. Their use was however restricted to within the Turkish community. In general use were the place names taken over from British colonial times when Cyprus became a Republic in 1960. These were usually the Greek historical place names but in some instances – in the case of Nicosia, for example, which goes back to Venetian times – the place names have been taken from European usage rather than Greek or Turkish: Nicosia is known as Lefkosia by the Greeks and Lefkoşa by the Turks. We have

kept here to the approved version. New Turkish names are only given in brackets where this is necessary in order to find the places. The numbers before each place name refer to the relevant number on the map on page 138.

(1) **Ayia Napa:** once an idyllic village lying among windmills, fertile fields and white sandy beaches on the south-eastern tip of Cyprus, but today overrun by tourism, which only took hold here after 1974. It is especially sought after by Scandinavian, German and British tour groups. In the middle of the village is a monastery going back to Venetian times in the 16th century, and a chapel which is used by the local inhabitants as the village church. The complex has been an ecumenical centre since 1978.

(2) **Alasia:** the ruins of a Bronze Age city which at the time was on the coast, near the village of Engomi, north of Famagusta. The site is often known as "Engomi" after the nearby village. The excavations, which were begun in the '30s, brought marvellous finds to light, including the bronze horned god from the 12th century B.C. which is to be found in the museum in Nicosia. Alasia had 15,000 inhabitants at its peak period around the middle of the second millenium B.C. It was considered the capital of Cyprus and the most important trading centre between the Orient and the Aegean. The impressive ruins are in what is today the Turkish-controlled north. The excavations, which are not yet complete, had to be broken off in 1974, and the site is now abandoned.

(3) **Amathus:** excavations, which are still in the early stages, of the ancient site of the same name about eight kilometres east of Limassol on the road to Nicosia. Amathus was one of the city kingdoms of Cyprus and was only overtaken by the rise of Limassol in the Middle Ages. It then rapidly lost importance. The remains of the acropolis are at the top of the hill, the climb is beautiful and worth the effort. Richard the Lionheart landed near Amathus in 1191 when he had to break his journey during the Third Crusade because of a storm.

(4) **Asinou:** the Church of the Virgin of the Fields, *Panayia Phorviotissa*, about five kilometres from the village of Nikitari on the northern wooded slopes of the Troodos mountains. This modest-looking church, with the characteristic gabled roof which is also to be found on other churches and monasteries in Cyprus, stands in the middle of the countryside and was once the centre of a monastery. It was built about 1105/1106 A.D. and the interior is almost entirely covered by frescoes, which date from the 12th to 14th centuries. To reach Asinou you take the road to Troodos from Nicosia and turn south off the main road at Kato Koutraphas to Nikitari. There you have to find the village priest and take him with you to Asinou. He has the key to this isolated church standing in the middle of forests and fields.

(5) **The Baths of Aphrodite:** this grotto lies about ten kilometres west of Polis. Surrounded by lush vegetation, the spring gushes out of the rocks all the year round. The spot is connected with the Goddess of Love Aphrodite, at least according to verbal tradition. There is no historical evidence for this, however. Perhaps the untouched beauty of the region brought about the legend. On the way to the grotto (via a footpath) there is a tourist pavilion overlooking the sea. Anyone who decides to go on further will, after about eight kilometres' walk, come upon a well known as the *Fontana Amorosa*, the spring of love. According to the old reports, anyone who drank from the spring would fall in love. Today it is often used as a watering-place for sheep. It is forbidden to build streets or houses in this area and there are plans to make it into a wild life reserve.

(6) **Bellapais Abbey:** these ruins of the monastery founded in the 13th century under the Lusignan by Roman Catholic monks (White Friars) are the most beautiful Gothic buildings in Cyprus. The present name comes from the original name *Abbaye de la Paix*, Abbey of Peace. In 1570 it was destroyed by the Turks. In the remains of the monastery church the Greek population of the village (which is also called Bellapais) used to hold services. In 1974/75 the whole population of the village had to leave Bellapais, and Turkish Cypriots from the south of the island settled there. The church is now closed but it is still possible to visit the ruins of the abbey, from which there is a marvellous view down to Kyrenia, and on clear days one can even see the snow-covered caps of the Taurus mountains in Turkey. The refectory and the cloister are largely intact. The English author Lawrence Durrell lived in Bellapais in the '50s and wrote one of the most evocative books on Cyprus, "Bitter Lemons".

(7) **Buffavento:** one of the three castles on the Kyrenia mountain range built by the Byzantines in the 10th century as fortifications against the Arab invasions. They were later added to by the Lusignans but abandoned during Turkish times. The remains of the walls near Pentadaktylos, the "five finger mountain", can be reached by a mountain path from Bellapais. The ascent is also possible from the summit of the highway east of Kyrenia which goes over the mountain range. It is best to make enquiries in advance, as the whole mountain range is crisscrossed with military areas which are off-limits.

Engomi: see Alasia

(8) **Famagusta:** the third largest town in Cyprus with an important port. The old town is surrounded by an impressive Venetian wall and has been inhabited solely by Turks since the Turkish conquest in 1571. The old town contains the ruins of Famagusta's golden age period under the Lusignan and Venetians. The Gothic Cathedral of St. Nicholas (built between 1298 and 1326) was turned into a mosque in 1571. Since then it has been known by the name of the Turkish conqueror, Lala Mustapha. A minaret, which looks as if it had been clipped on, tells of the changing fortunes and times. Once Famagusta was the richest town in the whole of the Levant because of trade. Its rise was the result of the arrival of Christian refugees from Palestine after the fall of Akko in 1291. It is said, that nobleman at the time used to season their food with ground jewels.

From 1274 to 1464 the town belonged to the Republic of Genoa, then after 1489 it came under Venetian rule like the rest of Cyprus. Inside the walls of the city there are said to have been 365 churches and countless luxurious palaces belonging to the leading families.

In the cathedral which is today the *Lala Mustapha Mosque*, the Lusignan kings were crowned "Kings of Cyprus and Jerusalem". The town decayed after its conquest by the Turks. The Greek Orthodox population had to leave, and settled outside the town walls. This new town was known as "Varosha" or "suburb", while the Greeks today call Famagusta "Ammohostos", which means "hidden in the sand". Stones

from old Famagusta were taken to build the Suez Canal and Port Said, just as Famagusta itself was once partly built out of the ruins of Salamis.

Apart from the mosque, the city walls, on which one can partially circle the town, are well worth a visit. The walls include the citadel known as *Othello's Tower* with the winged Lion of St. Mark over the entrance (which is the venue for Shakespears's tragedy "Othello"), and the *Djamboulat Bastion*. The bastion is called after a Turkish officer who is buried there and revered as a saint by the Turks. During the siege he is supposed to have put one of the defensive weapons of the Venetians out of action by riding into it with his horse and being cut to pieces. In the bastion is a small museum with Turkish weapons.

Opposite the Lala Mustapha Mosque, one can see the remains of the *Venetian Palace* from where the Lusignan and later the Venetians and Genoese ruled the city and perhaps the whole island. It was also known as the *Palazzo del Provveditore*. In Turkish times it served as a prison, while Famagusta – which the Turks called "Magoşa" after the conquest – was notorious as a place of exile. At the entrance to the mosque opposite, Turkish Cypriots have erected a monument to the Turkish national poet Namik Kemal Bey, who was imprisoned here from 1873 to 1876 because he challenged the Sultan.

By 1974 the old and new towns of Famagusta together had about 45,000 inhabitants. Today only the outskirts of the new town are inhabited by Turkish Cypriots. The Greek Cypriots fled in 1974 from the booming tourist mecca, which was one of the main earners of foreign currency. The largest part of the town is today uninhabited and off-limits except to the Turkish army, and is rotting gradually in the sun and salty wind – a ghost town.

(9) **Hala Sultan Tekke:** located on the Salt Lake near Larnaca, this was once a Dervish monastery with a mosque which contains the grave of Umm Haram, who is considered by many to be the aunt of the Prophet Mohammed. In fact she was the aunt of his private secretary and died here in 647 A.D. when she fell off a mule during an Arab invasion of Cyprus. Her grave was only found centuries later and a mosque was built over it in Turkish times. Hala Sultan Tekke is an important holy place for Muslims and is considered by many pilgrims the fourth holy place, ranking after Mecca, Medina, and the Dome of the Rock in Jerusalem.

(10) **Saint Hilarion:** the most important, and biggest, of the three Byzantine fortifications on the Kyrenia range, named after a hermit, Hilarion, who is supposed to have died here in the 16th century. The fortification of St. Hilarion was also extended by the Lusignan and later taken over by the Venetians. From here one can see the whole mountain range. Fire signals were used to send messages between Buffavento and Kantara, the easternmost of the three castles, and St. Hilarion. After 1570 the fortress was occupied by the Turks.

In the three levels which are built one on top of the other, one can clearly discern three elements: the lowest level is the arsenal and barracks for the guard, above that is the Byzantine church from the 10th century, which is named after Hilarion, and – as crowning glory – the manorial palace.

During the struggle between Greek and Turkish Cypriots in 1963/64, the Turks took the fortress to protect the flank of their enclave in the north of Nicosia. It was for many years a military post but is now open to the public again. When one approaches St. Hilarion it looks like the palace of Sleeping Beauty. The view down to the sea and to Kyrenia is one of the most splendid in Cyprus.

(11) **Kakopetria:** a small, idyllically located village on the northern slopes of the Troodos mountains, popular as a summer resort and known for its fruit, especially apples, cherries and peaches. A whole section of the old village is subject to a preservation order and is being lovingly restored at the moment. Worth seeing is the church of *Ayios*

explanation of the burial rituals, are to be found in the Cyprus Museum in Nicosia.

(15) **Kiti:** about ten kilometres from Larnaca. The village church of Panayia Angeloktistos, which means "built by the angels", dates from the 10th to 11th centuries, the chapel at the entrance from the 14th century. The middle section is supposed to be built on the ruins of a Byzantine church, which explains the origin of the mosaic in the apse, the oldest and most beautiful to be found in Cyprus. It was taken from the previous building and dates from the 6th or 7th century and shows the Virgin and Christ Child flanked by the archangels Michael and Gabriel. During museum opening hours a custodian is on duty, so one does not have to search for the key in the village.

Monasteries: Cyprus still has many monasteries in which monks and nuns of the Orthodox Church live and work. They were always places of pilgrimage and there is usually a legend concerning a miracle connected with their foundation. They still play an important role in the religious but also economic life of Cyprus. The abbots are seen as advisers and father confessors, not only by the simple folk who come to them with their problems, but also by the middle-class townsfolk, and consequently they have great influence.

The monastery of **Ayios Neophytos** (16), located about eight kilometres outside Ktima (Paphos), goes back to the time of the hermit Neophytos who lived and worked here in a cave in the 12th century. He described and bemoaned the "misfortune of Cyprus". His cave is decorated with frescoes and can be visited. The relics of the saint are venerated in the monastery church, which has an iconostasis dating from the 16th century which is one of the most beautiful in Cyprus. Among the most important monasteries are: (17) **Chrysorrogiatissa**, near Pano Panayia, the birthplace of Archbishop Makarios, which is located in the Paphos district and which, like most of the monasteries, was founded in the 12th century. The name means monastery of "The Virgin Mary of the Mountain of the Golden Pomegranate". The treasure of the monastery is an icon of Mary, which a hermit who once lived here saw shining out at sea from this point. He thought it was an icon which could perform miracles and which the iconoclasts of Isauria in Asia Minor had thrown into the sea and that it had swum to Cyprus. He was told by the Virgin in a dream to build a chapel for the icon near his cave on Rogia (= pomegranate) mountain. The monastery later developed around this.

The name of the monastery also indicates the significance for Cyprus of the pomegranate, which is connected with the cult of Aphrodite.

Kykko monastery (18), situated high up in the Troodos mountains, is the most important in Cyprus. It contains an icon of Mary which is supposed to have been painted by the Evangelist Luke and given to the newly-founded monastery by the Byzantine Emperor Alexis Komnenos around 1100 A.D. The name of the monastery may be connected with the ebony trees which once grew here. The word "Kokkous" (ebony tree) may have been the origin of the present Kykko.

Kykko owned large areas of land in the Near East and as far afield as Russia. Even today it is the richest monastery in the island, a fact which the visitor can easily deduce from the use of shining marble everywhere.

In view of its land-holdings and the blocks of flats built by the monastery, for example in Nicosia, the monastery is also an economic force. Makarios was a novice here, and the EOKA leader Grivas directed his struggle against the British from here for a while. His guerrilla fighters found refuge here disguised as monks. Above Kykko, at the top of the mountain Throni, Archbishop Makarios is buried in a simple chapel of stone hewn from the region.

The **monastery of Makheras** (19) lies about forty kilometres southwest of Nicosia in a beautiful area of woods. Here too there is an icon which is supposed to work miracles, as well as a knife which is supposed to have given the monastery its name (mahairi = knife), and which is

Nicolaos with Byzantine frescoes dating from the 10th to the 17th century.

A visit to Kakopetria is also worthwile for gourmets; they will enjoy fresh local trout and other local delicatessen.

(12) **Kalopanayiotis:** the monastery of Ayios Ioannis Lampadistis "the enlightener" lies outside this picturesque mountain village, which hangs onto the side of the Troodos mountains. The oldest part of the church, which was built in three parts, dates from the 11th century; various other sections were added in the following centuries. In addition to the main church, which is decorated with frecoes, there are two side chapels. In one the grave of the saint is to be found; he was a deacon here and is said to have performed various miracles. During the usual working hours for museums, the village priest will take visitors into the church, which is otherwise closed. The church is worth the effort and patience required to find the priest and the keys.

(13) **Kantara:** the easternmost castle of the Byzantine string of fortification along the Kyrenia mountain range. Today it is once more open to the public after being closed as a military area by the Turkish army. From Kantara one can see along the coast as far as the Carpass peninsula as well as inland over the Mesaoria plain, as far as Famagusta. What is left of the fortifications probably dates from the 14th century. In the small nearby village of Kantara, the Orthodox *monastery of Kantariotissa* was to be found in Lusignan times. It was famous as a centre of resistance against the oppression of the Roman Church.

(14) **Khirokitia:** located on the road between Nicosia and Limassol about five kilometres after the turning for Lefkara, this is the oldest Stone Age settlement in Cyprus, some 8000 years old. The remains of the circular houses climb up the steep mountainside. The finds and the burial chambers located under the circular houses, along with an

The richest monastery in Cyprus: ↓kko in the Troodos mountains (left).

The monastery of Makheras, southwest of Nicosia, which originates from the 12th century.

middle of a Turkish military area. The Carpass peninsula is off-limits to foreigners – unfortunately; because it is one of the most beautiful, unspoiled areas of Cyprus.

The origins of the monastery go back to early Christian times. St. Andrew, the Apostle and brother of St. Peter, stopped off here on one of his missionary journeys from Jerusalem. The ship had run out of drinking water and Andrew told the sailors to put in to land, where they would find a clear spring. In thanks for having been saved, the captain later brought a picture of the saint back to the place, and so the monastery was founded. Every year on the 15th August and 30th November, thousands of Greek Cypriots would make the pilgrimage to St. Andreas. They would bring the sick and infirm with them hoping that they would be healed. Very often pious Muslims would make the pilgrimage as well.

The **monastery of St. Barnabas** (23) near Salamis is also very important in the annals of the history of the Greek Orthodox Church. Barnabas,

who accompanied the Apostle Paul on his travels, is the patron saint of the island. He was born in Salamis, and after missionary work in Cyprus became the first bishop of the area and died a martyr's death here. He is considered to be the founder of the Cypriot Church.

When the grave, with his bones and a copy of the Gospel according to St. Matthew in Barnabas' own hand, was found four hundred years later, in 478 A.D., a dream apparition was again in play: in a dream, Barnabas told Archbishop Anthimos, who was fighting for the independence of the Cypriot Church from the Patriarch of Antioch, where the grave was to be found. Anthimos found it and travelled with the "Barnabas copy" of the Gospel according to St. Matthew to Emperor Zeno in Constantinople, who gave the Cypriot Church its independence. Since then it has been autocephalous, its Archbishop is not answerable to any of the Eastern Patriarchs and still today enjoys certain privileges granted by Zeno – he is allowed to sign in red ink and to wear an imperial purple cloak and carry a sceptre.

The church which was built over the grave of Barnabas in the 5th century was shortly afterwards destroyed by the Arabs. The present-day monastery dates from the 18th century, and contains some sections built in the 10th century. Today it is a museum. The monks, who were known and loved for their reproductions of icons, had to leave their home in 1974 when the area came under Turkish control. The location of the grave is marked by a small chapel erected in the '50s and lies opposite the main entrance to the monastery.

The monastery of **St. Chrysostomos** (24), on the southern slopes of the Kyrenia mountains overlooking the Mesaoria plain, is today a Turkish military camp. Before 1974, Greek troops were stationed here. Its position in a forest about 600 metres above sea level, with a wonderful view over the plain to Nicosia, made it a popular destination for excursions for people from Nicosia. Here, too, a spring with healing powers was the reason for founding the monastery, which most recently belonged to the Greek Orthodox Patriarch of Jerusalem. The

said to have been found in a cave. Makheras also played a part in the resistance against the British.

Grivas' deputy, Grigoris Afxentiou was burned to death in a cave beneath the monastery. For many Greek Cypriots the location of the gruesome events is a place of pilgrimage.

Stavrovouni monastery (20) (Stavrovouni = mountain of the cross), is supposed to have been built by St. Helena, the mother of the Emperor Constantine, in 327 A.D. on her return journey from the Holy Land. She brought a piece of the true cross with her, which is still venerated today in Stavrovouni. Since then it has been one of the most important places of pilgrimage on the island and it is the monastery with the most conservative ideas and strictest rules. Women have recently been banned from entering the monastery, and exceptions are only made on Sundays.

The monks work hard on the steep slopes and on an agricultural holding at the foot of the mountain. The honey of Stavrovouni which is sold there is excellent. There is also an icon-painter in residence who will gladly show his work.

Trooditissa monastery (21) lies on the southern slopes of the Troodos mountains, and is dedicated to the Holy Virgin Mary of the Troodos Mountains. Here, too, the Virgin is supposed to have appeared to two monks in a dream and to have told them to build a church.

Inside the monastery the so-called "holy belt" is to be found. Women who want a son wear the belt while they pray and promise the son to the monastery. This promise can be redeemed by the payment of money or goods, usually a donation of fields or fruit-bearing trees which add to the monastery's property.

Three of the most important monasteries for the Greeks now lie in the Turkish-controlled area of the north and so cannot be visited by them: **Apostolos Andreas monastery** (22), a national shrine for the Orthodox Church of Cyprus, lies at the tip of the Carpass peninsula, in the two churches inside the monastery are dedicated to the saints Chryso-stomos and John, a Patriarch of Alexandria who came from Cyprus.

In all monasteries in the south, hikers and travellers can spend the night free of charge. The cells are simple, usually without running water, but clean. Everyone is expected to make a donation before leaving the next day. For anyone who wants to combine the pleasures of the Troodos mountain landscape with the Byzantine world of the monasteries, a hike from one monastery to another between Polis and Paphos, including some of the lesser-known ones such as Ayii Anargyri – known for the holy doctors Kosmas and Damian who treated their patients free of charge, hence the name "saints without money" – is a very special Cypriot experience.

(25) Kolossi: this tower-like fortification lies on the edge of the village of the same name in the middle of extensive vineyards, and was for a long time the headquarters of the Commander-in-chief of the Knights Templar. What is left of the structure today dates from the middle of the 15th century. One can climb the winding staircase through the various levels made up of halls and towers until one reaches an open-air platform from where one has a wonderful view of what was once the commander's domain.

Next to the fort stands what once was a sugar factory, a hall with Gothic arches. Until the discovery of the New World, sugar cane was cultivated in Cyprus. The fertile region around Kolossi was especially well-known for this. The heavy sweet dessert wine made from the grapes around the castle has till today kept its name "Commandaria" after the commanding officer of those days. It is possible to visit the complex during normal museum opening times.

(26) Kouklia (Old Paphos): this small village overlooking the road from Limassol to Paphos was built on the ruins of Old Paphos, which was the centre of the cult of Aphrodite for the ancient world. Excava-tions have been going on here since the end of the 19th century. So far the foundations of a huge complex have been found, including – in recent years – the foundations of the Temple of Aphrodite from the late Bronze Age as well as a later Roman temple which has been excavated by German and Swiss archaeologists. It is believed that the whole complex was much larger and that some of it lies under the present village. In one of the Lusignan forticiations a museum has been established.

The church of *Panayia Katholiki*, which is situated on the edge of the excavations near the road, is well worth seeing because of its frescoes, but is unfortunately usually closed. (The key is with the village priest, who is often to be found in one or the other village "kafenion".)

(27) Kourion (Curium): an important site and one of the most important places in ancient Cyprus, with a unique position high above the sea on the road from Limassol to Paphos. Kourion, probably founded in the 12th century B.C. by Greek emigrants from Argolis, was famous for its temple and oracle and exercised great influence because of this well into the Christian era. The town probably had about 25,000 inhabitants at its height. The remaining ruins, which include a Roman bath with floor mosaics, an amphitheatre used in summer for perfor-mances (it is a unique experience to sit under the star-studded sky high above the dark sea) and an early Christian basilica, all date from early Christian times.

A bit further along the road to Paphos, on the right-hand side, lies the stadium of the ancient town and the *Apollo-Hylates Temple* which has been excavated. "Apollo of the woods" was the protector of Kourion.

Kourion was one of the most famous places of pilgrimage, second only to the Temple of Aphrodite at Paphos which is not far from here. The forests which once covered this region have now disappeared. Kourion today lies in the middle of Mediterranean scrubland, through which the rocky earth can be seen. When one looks inland from the Apollo Temple, one sees another sort of forest – a forest of

antennae from the British military base Akrotiri on which Kourion is situated.

(28) Kyrenia (Turkish *Girne*): this little town built around a horseshoe harbour on the north coast of Cyprus, is a jewel. The prehistory of Kyrenia goes back to neolithic times. It was one of the city-kingdoms of the island and under the Byzantines it was integrated into the defensive system of the Kyrenia mountain range along with St. Hilarion, Buff-avento and Kantara.

The *fort* was extended by the Lusignan and later strengthened by the Venetians. In 1570 it surrendered to the Turks without a struggle; the Turks, incidentally, landed near Kyrenia in 1974 as well.

Today the castle houses the Shipwreck Museum, after having been used as a prison in British colonial times for EOKA fighters among others. The museum can boast a unique find: a trading ship from the time of Alexander the Great, loaded with goods, which was coming from Rhodes and sank off the coast of Kyrenia around 300 B.C. It was found by chance by a local diver in 1967 and later brought up piece by piece, including the amphorae, and reassembled. The work was carried out by an American team of deep sea archaeologists under the super-vision of Michael Katzev. The hulk of the ship, which is around 12 metres long and 4.5 metres wide, can be visited during normal museum opening hours.

Kyrenia, which lies in the most beautiful and – for West Europeans – culturally rich part of the island, quickly became a favourite place of retirement after the Second World War for ex-colonial civil servants who at the end of their period of service did not want to return to the rain and fog of Great Britain. Many have stayed on even after 1974 because they would otherwise have had to reckon with the loss of their homes. Many of them knew the British diplomat and writer Lawrence Durrell, who in "Bitter Lemons" describes how this paradise was shattered in the fifties by growing political unrest.

The villages around Kyrenia, especially *Bellapais, Kazaphani, Karmi* and *Lapithos*, are among the most beautiful in Cyprus. The plentiful water supplies provide the basis for rich citrus fruit plantations.

Kyrenia and its surroundings have about 5000 inhabitants, that is fewer than before 1974. They are Turkish Cypriots from the south of the island who have moved into the houses of the Greek Cypriots who fled or were forced out after 1974. Kyrenia, which was once a holiday paradise and an ideal environment for artists to work in, is now much quieter than it used to be. The presence of the Turkish army everywhere and the many military zones along the beautiful coast at the foot of the mountains are depressing factors. Even the Turkish Cypriots who were originally from Kyrenia, which always had a Turkish community of a few hundred, and those who live in the surrounding villages, bemoan the fact. It prevents their efforts to recreate the old days in spite of the present political situation.

(29) Lagoudhera: this unique village in the Pitsilia mountains on the northern slopes of the Troodos range and its monastery church *Panayia tou Arakos* – Our Lady of Arakos – are worth the 65-kilometres trip from Nicosia. It is easiest to reach from the Troodos road where one turns off to the left at Peristerona and continues in the direction of Kato Moni as far as Polystipos. From there it is about five kilometres to the church.

The frescoes, which date from the year 1192 A.D., are the most beautiful and best-preserved examples of Byzantine art in Cyprus. They are influenced by the Italian Renaissance and have recently been restored by a team of American experts so that one can now get their full effect, freed from candle grease. The key to the church is with the village priest.

(30) Larnaca: was built by the Byzantines in the early Middle Age and is today the fourth largest town in the island, with 25,000 inhabitants. It lies on the location of the ancient Kition, one of the city-kingdoms of Cyprus. Kition is mentioned in the Bible as Kittim. It was an

Continued on page 133

The Lala Musta-
pha Mosque in
Famagusta, origi-
nally the Cathedral
of St. Nicholas
which was begun in
1298, is a purely
Gothic building. The
unity of style has
been detracted from
by the minarets
added in 1571.

A view of Peristerona. In the background, the Troodos mountains.

The courtyard of Ayia Napa monastery.

The fort in the harbour of Paphos.

Overleaf: in the Church of Ayios Mamas in Morphou.

Kourion, probably founded by immigrants from Argolis in the 12th century B.C., has a unique position overlooking the sea east of Limassol.

Mosaics from Kourion (top right and left, middle left and bottom left), and from Soli (middle right and bottom right).

131

The remains of the cloisters in Bellapaïs Abbey, south-east of Kyrenia.

important Phoenician trading settlement. The recent excavations under Dr. Karageorgis, the Director of the Department of Antiquities in Cyprus, have brought to light interesting information on this aspect of the city's past.

The excavations of ancient Kition – which are in the middle of disorganised and rapidly expanding Larnaca – are open to the public. The main finds are in the town museum, but some are also in the Nicosia Museum.

St. Lazarus' Church, with the sarcophagus of the saint, is the monument with which Larnaca's present name is connected (Larnax = sarcophagus). It was built at the end of the 9th century when Lazarus' grave was discovered. Lazarus is supposed to have lived his second life after his resurrection in Cyprus – as the first Bishop of Larnaca.

Another must is the *house of the Swedish Consul Pierides*, with its unique collection of antique finds, which is now open to the public. It is located near the customs house and police station, and has the typical architecture of a bygone era, when Larnaca was more important than it is today.

During Turkish times, as the Famagusta harbour fell into disuse, Larnaca with its relatively flat sea bed was a good landing place for trading ships. People were disembarked a little way out and carried ashore. Nearly all goods which were brought to or sent out of the island were dealt with here in this way. In order to protect their salesmen and officers, the European powers set up consulates in Larnaca, and the town is still today proud of its name as "the city of consuls".

Larnaca is once again gaining ground as a trade centre, with the international airport which was built up from an old British military landing strip after 1974 (the larger international airport in Nicosia has been out of use since the Turkish invasion of 1974, and is only open to the United Nations), and the harbour which has been rebuilt following the invasion. The arrival of thousands of refugees has led to the development of many new industries, particularly in the clothing sector. Its clothing plants are very successful in exporting their products to Western Europe.

Every year at Whitsun, Larnaca celebrates the *festival of Kataklysmos*, a colourful fair with a programme of songs and dances and the appearance of folk poets who recite the folk songs and poems of Cyprus. This festival may be connected with the earlier cult of Aphrodite. The Church of Cyprus celebrates the great flood but, as is so often the case, the old heathen rituals and the Christian ones have blended together so that when the people flock to the seafront together they are celebrating the birth of Aphrodite from the foam, even if they do not know it.

(31) **Lefkara:** a village lying on the south-east foothills of the Troodos mountains. Popular as a summer resort and easy to reach from the Nicosia-Limassol road. The women of the village make the famous Lefkara lace and embroidery. They sit together in groups in the narrow lanes during the cool evenings, and one can see them at their work. This custom is said to go back to the ladies of Venetian times who came here to escape the heat of Nicosia and whiled away their spare time with embroidery.

Embroidery has made Lefkara prosperous and the prices for the famous "Lefkaritika", which is exported all over the world, rise openly in unison with the rise in tourism in Cyprus. Leonardo da Vinci is supposed to have taken Lefkara lace for the altar cloth of the Cathedral of Milan.

(32) **Limassol:** the most relaxed and jolly of the Cypriot towns. As a port town, it was always more open to new ideas and it has now taken over from Famagusta as a tourist centre. The town, which today has 70,000 inhabitants, goes back to Crusader times. In the old *castle*, which is the only monument of historical importance in this town which has always been forward-looking and future-orientated, Richard the Lionheart is supposed to have married his bride Berengaria of Navarre in 1191. The castle is today the city museum.

Limassol is known for its wine and spirits industry which is concentrated here. Visitors are always welcome in the wineries. Limassol is Cyprus' main port.

(33) **Morphou** (Turkish *Güzelyurt*): a small town on the edge of the Morphou bay, lying in the middle of extensive orange and lemon plantations. In mythical times there was a temple of Aphrodite here, and over the grave of St. Mamas a church was erected in the 12th century, which has been a museum since 1974.

A few kilometres' drive from Morphou, one can reach the remains of the ancient city of *Soli* which was built around 600 B.C. at the command of the philosopher Solon, with its Hellenistic-Roman amphitheatre carved out of the chalky stone, as well as the palace of Vouni a few kilometres further west, which overlooks the sea and which shows a strong oriental influence. It is believed to have been built by a member of a royal family from Marion to the west (which is today Polis) which was well-connected with Persia, in order to control the entrance to Soli. One can only visit these sites with special permission, which has to be obtained in the last village before Soli.

(34) **Nicosia** (Greek *Levkosia*; Turkish *Lefkoşa*): since 1960 the capital of the Republic of Cyprus and has remained – even after the partition of the town by the Green Line in 1963/64 following the unrest between Greeks and Turks – the commercial and administrative centre for both communities.

The town appears with the name Ledra as one of the city-kingdoms in the 7th century B.C., but probably there was already a late Bronze Age settlement here as early as the fourth millenium B.C. After it was fortified in 300 B.C. by the Ptolemy Levkos (which is the origin of the names today used by the Greeks and Turks), it quickly lost importance. It only regained the importance which it has maintained until today under the Lusignan. Ledra became the capital and seat of the Roman Catholic Archbishop.

The Venetians expanded the incomplete defensive system by building a wall around the city, which still encircles the town. The eleven bastions are named after the eleven commanders-in-chief. This is an impressive defensive complex, not only by Mediterranean standards.

The walls are today integrated into the life of the town, as there are parking places where the rural buses park and playgrounds where school children play basket-ball. Traffic runs along the walls, and in many places streets and rows of houses have been built on them. If it were not for the fact that one would have to cross the Green Line twice, a walk around the walls would be a fascinating trip through past and present.

The walls could not withstand the Turkish besiegers in 1570, who broke through at Constanza bastion. Even today a small mosque commemorates the spot, the *Bayraktar* (standardbearer) *Mosque* (A). It was partially destroyed by Greek EOKA fanatics in the '60s. The Turkish conquerors are said to have killed 20,000 people when they took the city, and the bloodbath lasted three days. It therefore took some time before the Greek population of the city could bring itself up to the same numerical level as the Turkish population which settled there.

Today Nicosia has two totally different faces: the bustling commercial life of the Greek side, which is rapidly expanding with the construction of new apartment blocks on the outskirts of the town, not always to the city's advantage, contrasting with the slower, more relaxed pace of the Turkish side for whom liveliness and progress are not the most important goals in life – as they are for their neighbours on the other side.

The most important evidence of the city's past is today to be found on the Turkish side. What was once the Gothic *Cathedral of St. Sophia* (B) is today called the Selimiye Mosque, named after Sultan Selim II under whom Cyprus became Turkish. It has been transformed by two minarets, like Famagusta Cathedral. The interior decoration has been removed and the walls have been whitewashed. It is the main mosque in the Turkish area of Nicosia.

Next to this is another partially destroyed building, formerly the *St. Nicholas Church* and later a covered market, the *Bedestan* (C) (= covered bazaar). Here cloth goods were sold during Turkish times.

Another Gothic building from Lusignan times, *St. Katherine's Church* became the *Haydar Pasha Mosque* (D). It is today so structurally unsound that it can no longer be visited.

Well worth seeing is the *Büyük Han* (E), the Large Inn. The building of inns and caravanserai was important in Turkish times since the trading caravans needed security and rest stops on their long journeys through the Ottoman Empire. The Büyük Han is a large square complex with two colonnades facing the interior courtyard around which there are sixty-eight rooms. In the middle of the courtyard is a

by Mustapha Kemal Pasha, later known as Atatürk. So their time came to an end under the Turkish Cypriots as well who, already influenced by the British, accepted Atatürk's goals for modernisation and Europeanisation quite early on. One could almost say that they understood him better than the Anatolian Turks, since to some extent they had already been part of Europe for fifty years.

In general, the Turkish side of Nicosia gives the impression of being historically richer and more compact. This is due to the different mentality and also the lack of money, so that the rebuilding which so violently interrupted the natural development of the city on the Greek side did not take place here. Here one gets a feeling of what life was like in the 19th century, in old Cyprus as it appears in the engravings and drawings of the "Illustrated London News" in the year 1878, while on the Greek side one has the feeling that the old is no longer appreciated.

mosque. The buildings are to be restored but the funds have yet to be found, so they are closed. One can however get permission to visit them from the relevant authority: the attendant on duty can tell you where to go, and it is well worth doing this.

Opposite this complex lies a smaller one (F), the *Kumarcilar Han*, the Inn of the Gamblers. It has been largely restored and houses the Department of Antiquities, from which one can get permission to visit the Büyük Han. The Turkish Cypriots are especially helpful and hospitable and will always try and satisfy the tourist's wishes. If this has not always been possible since 1974, it is not their fault: they are also victims of the absurd political situation.

Next to what was once Kyrenia Gate, the *Turkish Cypriot Ethnographic Museum* is housed in what used to be the *Monastery of the Dancing Dervishes* (G). It boasts many treasures both artistic and from daily life including important firmans, that is decrees of the Sultan concerning Cyprus, and the personal Koran of the Commander-in-chief Lala Mustapha. One should definitely include a visit to this small but significant museum when in the Turkish area of Nicosia in order to understand why the Turkish Cypriots feel they have a valid right to consider Cyprus as their homeland. Their religion and their culture have influenced the island for over three hundred years. The picture that they have of themselves is not that of a minority, but of an independent separate community.

The Mevlevi Dervishes, also known as the Dancing Dervishes, who practised in this one-time monastery were outlawed in Turkey in 1925

However, in recent years on the Greek side they are trying to reverse the results of unplanned development. There are two examples of this which the visitor to Nicosia should definitely see. Both are due to the initiative of the Municipal Council and the long-standing mayor of Nicosia, Lellos Demetriades, who has a great interest in the cultural heritage of Nicosia – the whole of Nicosia. The Famagusta Gate entrance to the Venetian walls, which was dilapidated and closed, has been restored and is now used as an exhibition, lecture and concert hall. This was an attempt to bring life to this part of the town near the Green Line, but is also evidence of a new cultural self-awareness on the Greek side.

The second example is the restored area of Nicosia, the entrance to which is to be found opposite the main post office. It is called *Laiki Yitonia*, which means something like "people's neighbourhood", and the old Cypriot tradition of "Kopiaste" or "please do come in" is reflected in taverns, coffee-shops and shops. It is true that this mentality was never really lost by the Greeks, only the rapid change on the exterior led to a neglect of the old architectural styles. The town has accepted this new quarter in the old-world style and one can only hope that this initiative will set a new trend.

The *Cyprus Museum* (H) in the Greek area of the town provides a vivid and systematically arranged review of Cyprus' classical history. Here one can see all the cultural and artistic developments of this Mediterranean island from Prehistoric to Roman times. The museum building, which dates from British colonial times (1908), is distinctive although the space is no longer adequate to exhibit all that is worth exhibiting. Here one comes across the remains of an early sanctuary, a find from the year 2000 B.C., in which a secret ritual was performed, here one can see the show-pieces of Cyprus' past, for example the colourful rhyton (a pointed-shaped drinking cup) from Kition, the horned god from Engomi, the marble statue of the Goddess Aphrodite from Soli, the finds from the graves of the kings near Salamis and the many small things which in those days influenced life so much more, and which in their often realistic beauty impress us so much today.

The collection of Cypriot terracottas, small clay figures which represent idols or simply the scenes of everyday life such as baking bread or giving birth in the upright position – which was usual until a few years ago in the villages in Cyprus – is unique, and for those who can find the greatest meaning in the smallest things and the present in the past, it is perhaps the most impressive thing of all in this exceptionally interesting museum.

Two other museums in the Greek part of the town are worth a visit. In a new building in the Archbishopric one comes upon the *Byzantine Museum* (I), which has been built with money collected by the Church over many years and which houses the most valuable and beautiful Cypriot icons. The exhibition in the new, light and well-arranged

the Sultan, before whom he was allowed to appear personally. As the Turkish population of Cyprus rose against the Sultan in 1804 on the grounds that the Turkish Governor was only a puppet in the hands of the Dragoman and the Archbishop, the Sultan ordered the rebellion to be put down by Hadji Georgakis Kornessios and thus the Sultan's intervention was in fact to the benefit of the Greek community.

This shows just how important their economic activity and tax contributions were, even to the Sultan residing so far away in Constantinople.

The prefix "Hadji" (= pilgrim) before a name is still to be found today in Cyprus. The Christians did not want to be outdone by the Muslims who used this prefix on returning from a pilgrimage to Mecca, so every Greek who had been on a pilgrimage to the Holy Land and Jerusalem adopted this prefix as well.

A map of Nicosia from 1580, and an aerial view of Nicosia from 1973. The Venetian fortifications have lasted till today.

rooms is not overcrowded. One is astounded by the abundance of Byzantine painting this island has produced, and for anyone who is not able to visit all the locations where Byzantine art is to be found in Cyprus, this museum offers an exceptional collection.

Also worth seeing is a collection of drawings, documents and paintings on the Greek War of Independence 1821–1829, which is exhibited on the third floor of the museum.

Right next to this building is the old Archbishopric – a typically Cypriot building with Gothic arches and verandahs, a style which was used for many years in the villages as well. It houses the Folk Art Museum (J) with well-chosen exhibits going back two hundred years. Many of the costumes can today only be seen in the museum and many of the customs, especially those to do with weddings, are now only to be found in remote areas.

Between the old and the new Archbishoprics (the new one was erected between 1956 and 1960 and is an uninteresting building in an ostentatious neo-Byzantine style) lies an architectural jewel: (K) *the Cathedral of St. John the Evangelist*. It is the Cathedral of the Archbishopric although the style and size are more reminiscent of a village church. There was an earlier church on this site but the present church dates from 1665, that is, it was built during Turkish times when all churches had to be lower than mosques. The frescoes are not so valuable, as they only date from the 18th century, but it is worth taking a look at the right-hand side: behind the carved wooden throne of the Archbishop, the story of the independence of the Church of Cyprus is depicted, just as it is on one of the walls in the monastery church of St. Barnabas.

In the same part of the town as the Archbishopric complex are a series of beautiful old houses dating from the 19th century, and in some cases even earlier, such as the *house of Hadji Georgakis Kornessios* (L). He occupied the post of Dragoman for a number of years and so was a sort of go-between or interpreter of the Greek community to the Court of

Besides the Church of *St. John* there are a number of other churches worth seeing in the Greek part of Nicosia. The best-known is *Phaneromeni Church* (M). It stands at the end of the main shopping streets, Ledra and Onassagorou, near the Green Line. Here in an annexe are to be found the remains of the priests who were slaughtered by the Turkish Governor in 1821.

A walk along the heavily guarded Green Line – which to some extent follows Hermes Street, the street of blacksmiths – is one impression that one should take back after a visit to this divided city. Sometimes one facade of a house is Greek and the other Turkish. Behind bricked-up windows, walls shot through with bullet holes, barbed wire fences, sandbags and oildrums, watchful soldiers keep an eye on one another. One should be careful when taking photographs – you will be stopped and the film will be confiscated, over this the Greeks and Turks are fully united. A photo of the rear view of one of the barricades could come into the hands of the enemy via Germany and give the enemy useful information – this kind of thinking, in an age of satellite photos which have already mapped out the whole world, makes it clear why the Cypriots on both sides are hopelessly stuck in a dead end.

(35) **Paphos** (New Paphos or Ktima): not to be confused with Old Paphos and the temple of Aphrodite which is today Kouklia, Paphos was founded in the Middle Ages on the same location as the Roman town of the same name. Until 1974 Paphos was outside the mainstream of life on the island. The upper town, Ktima, which has a strong Turkish element (the Turkish Cypriot politician Denktash was born and grew up here), attracted the life of the region as a market centre and then sent it back to the idyllic surrounding villages. Below in the fishing harbour of New Paphos, the small castle built by the Turks stood sentinel in the dusk, as did the remains of the pillars in front of *Chrysopolitissa Church*. St. Paul is said to have been bound to one of these pillars and beaten.

135

Paphos was always so cut off from the mainstream of events that it took a full ten years before the British Governor visited it for the first time after the British took control of the island. The war in 1974 changed all that overnight and the town now has ten years of tourist development behind it. Those tourists who want to concentrate on art and nature prefer it to the sterile tourist ghettos of Limassol and Ayia Napa.

In fact, even the garden town of New Paphos is now being taken over by souvenir shops, bars and fast-food restaurants. The once sleepy harbour has become a place for foolhardy village youths to show off their noisy motor-bikes. However, it is still possible to avoid all this. Long walks along the sea and in the interior are to be recommended, especially towards the north in the direction of Coral Bay.

The excavations, which had started before 1974 but are now being expedited, have made Paphos a treasure chest of art. The mosaics in the so-called *Villa of Dionysos* are the most beautiful dating from Roman times. The house is named for the God of Wine because he appears in so many of the mosaics. One of the large mosaics tells the story of how wine came to man: Dionysos, accompanied by the nymph Akme, teaches the legendary Athenian King Ikarios how to grow grapes. He in turn leaves the scene pulling an ox-cart laden with goatskins filled with wine. In the right-hand corner of the mosaic are two tipplers, who are described as the first wine-drinkers, visibly intoxicated. The legend which has come down to us, however, is not such a happy one: as Ikarios allowed them to drink the juice of the grape their heads started to spin and thinking that they had been poisoned by him, they murdered him.

Polish archaeologists are still carrying out excavations here. The most recently excavated mosaics are not yet open to the public, but are supposed to be the most beautiful in Cyprus. In the surrounding area there are many remains from Roman times, including the so-called "forty pillars" and a small amphitheatre.

On the coast road to the north, the *tombs of the kings* are to be found on the left-hand side: these are like a small subterranean city hewn out of rocks in which important and rich persons were buried in pre-Christian times. These graves seem to have been looted very early on. Later the early Christians found refuge here as well as in the extensive cave complex under the road stretching from Ktima to New Paphos – the two towns have now grown into one and are simply known as Paphos in everyday parlance. Here are to be found the cave of St. Solomoni and the grotto of the hermit Agapitikos.

The Chrysopolitissa Church was built in the 13th century and is situated in an impressive landscape of Roman and Byzantine ruins. This is where Christianity first took hold in Cyprus. St. Paul the Apostle converted the Roman Proconsul Sergius Paulus and so Cyprus became the first country to be ruled by a Christian.

Paphos is a perfect base for excursions into the western part of the island, which offers magical landscapes. *Polis*, the small fishing harbour of *Latchi*, *Kato Pyrgos* (which one can only visit by encircling a Turkish enclave via winding mountain roads, and which produces the tastiest figs in late summer) are all well worth a visit, as are many of the smaller, formerly often mixed, villages. One of them, Droushia, has all the atmosphere of a Cypriot "hill station".

(36) **Peristerona:** about thirty kilometres west of Nicosia on the road to Troodos, contains one of the earliest churches in Cyprus, from the 10th/11th centuries, dedicated to the saints Barnabas and Hilarion. With its five domes and three aisles the church symbolises the distinctive Byzantine style as it developed in Cyprus. There are, however, only a few frescoes left. But a short stop here is worthwhile for another reason: the church and the mosque standing next to one another, which was a fact of everyday life in Cyprus for so long, still exist here, although in fact only as an echo of the past. The Turkish inhabitants were forced to leave the village in 1964 by EOKA fanatics.

(37) **Platres:** in the middle of rich forests on the southern slopes of the Troodos mountains, a popular summer resort with many hotels and pensions. The view from here over the south of the island is splendid

Paphos harbour.

and Platres has a charm of its own as a holiday resort. One can walk for miles without meeting a soul. Beneath Platres lies the village of *Phini* which developed its own distinctive style of pottery-making centuries ago, but which is still a money-maker today.

(38) **Salamis:** situated on the coast north of Famagusta. A huge excavated city, over which the dust of a later age has been settling visibly since 1974. (It is clearly not their own historical past that the Turks are administering here.) The large amphitheatre from Roman times, with its 20,000 seats, is the largest so far discovered in Cyprus. In comparison, the gymnasium, the palaestra (school for wrestling), the baths and two market places which are stretched out between the pebbled beach and the park-like interior, are much more modest in size.

Salamis was the queen of the city-kingdoms on the island and benefited from its natural harbour and the diplomatic skills of its leaders, who managed to navigate between the interests of the Egyptians, Assyrians and Persians. In Roman times Salamis had more than 100,000 inhabitants. Under Byzantine rule the town experienced a renaissance under the name of Constantia, and then it was destroyed by earthquakes and by Arab invasions in the 7th century. The place became a quarry, and many columns, pillars and pieces of walls are still to be found today in the surrounding villages and in the old town to Famagusta.

The finds from the tombs known as the *Tombs of the Kings*, which were excavated in 1962 on the small road leading from Salamis to St. Barnabas' Monastery, the most important achievement in the career of the Cypriot archaeologist Dr. Karageorgis, were already mainly in the Nicosia museum even before 1974. It is still not clear to which kings the tombs relate. The quantity of the objects found and the skeletons of a team of horses and three slaves who were sacrificial victims, indicate a high-ranking personage of the 8th or 7th century before Christ.

(39) **Yeroskipos:** In this small village just outside Paphos, which most tourists just drive through, are two places of interest. First, the *Ayia Paraskevi Church* with its five domes in the Cypriot style from the 11th century, which is decorated inside with frescoes and icons, and second, the newly-established Folk Art Museum which is located in an old house in the middle of the village, which could not be more typically Cypriot. This was the office of a certain Andreas Zimboulakis who had emigrated from Kephalonia and who was the first official representative of Great Britain during the Napoleonic Wars when the British fleet appeared on the scene to back up the Army of the Nile.

The house was restored after 1978, and the former custodian of Kyrenia castle Yiannis Cleanthous has, with love and knowledge, turned it into one of the most beautiful museums in Cyprus. With very little money, he has collected an amazing number of old utensils, clothes, furniture and implements. Everything is well-displayed in the rooms in which the articles were originally used. One can spend hours making an ethnographic tour through a Cypriot house of the 19th century. In some villages off the beaten track, farmers still live in very much the same way.

This small museum, which unfortunately is easy to overlook, is as much a mirror of the soul of Cyprus as the mosaics, frescoes, temples and city walls. Yeroskipos means "holy garden": here once stood a temple to Aphrodite, and the pilgrims used to begin their festive, frolicking procession to Old Paphos from here.

137

CYPRUS

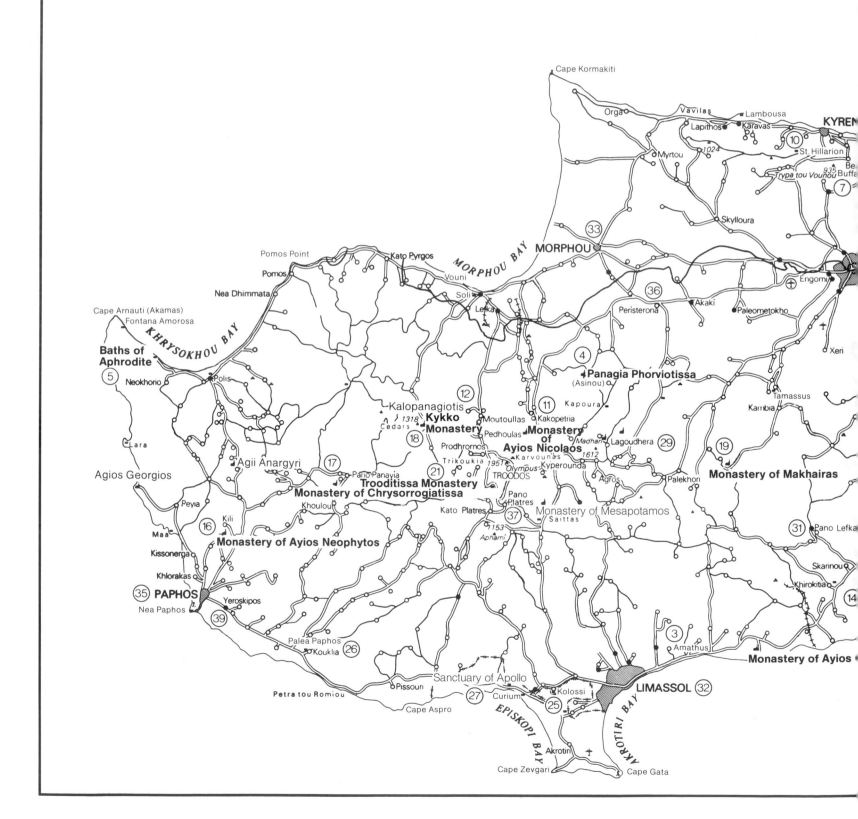

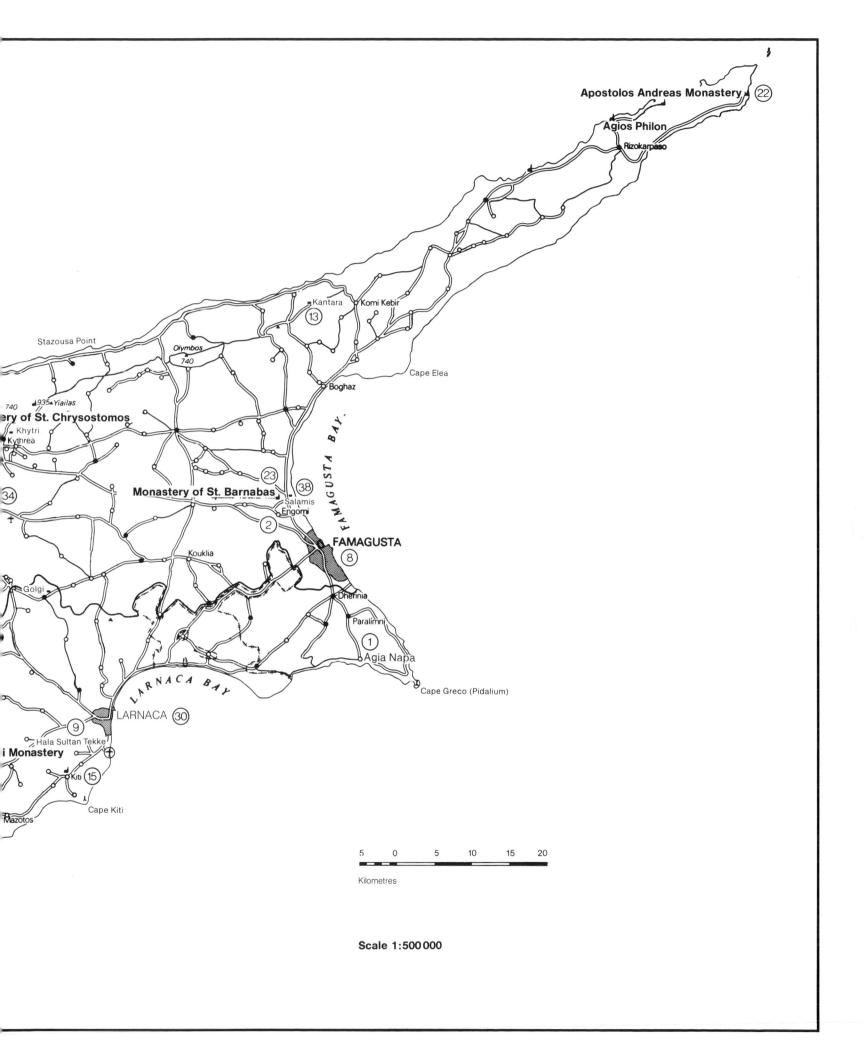

Index

Italic numbers refer to pictures.

List of Sources

Baybars, Taner: Plucked in a Far-off Land, London 1970.
Contemporary Cypriot Poetry, Nicosia 1981.
Delaval Cobham, Claude (Pub.): Excerpta Cypria – Materials for a History of Cyprus, New York 1969 (reprint of the 1908 edition).
Durrell, Lawrence: Bitter Lemons, Faber and Faber, London 1957.
Four Greek Poets, Penguin Books, London 1966.
Ludwig Salvator, Archduke of Austria: Levkosia, the capital of Cyprus, Trigraph, London 1981, reprinted from 1881 edition.

Mariti, Giovanni: Travels in the Island of Cyprus, London 1971 (reprint of the 1769 edition).
Merian Magazine 10/XXIII: "Zypern".
Niebuhr, Carsten: Entdeckungen im Orient – Reise nach Arabien und anderen Ländern 1761–1767, Tübingen 1973.
Poems of Cyprus, Nicosia 1970.
Thubron, Colin: Journey into Cyprus, 1971.
27 Centuries of Cypriot Poetry, Nicosia 1983.
Zarmas, Pieris: Studien zur Volksmusik Zypern, Baden-Baden 1975.

Byzantine Museum, Nicosia. Illustrations pp. 64, 65.
Cesnola, Louis Palma di: Cypern, seine alten Städte, Gräber und Tempel, bearbeitet von Ludwig Stern, Jena 1879. Illustrations pp. 98, 99.
Collection Lellos Demetriades, Nicosia. Illustrations pp. 7, 30, 31, 35, 55, 100, 101, 135 left.
Cyprus Museum, Nicosia. Illustrations pp. 66, 67, 73.
Gerster, Georg, Zumikon. Illustration p. 135 right.

Unger, F./Kotschy, Th.: Die Insel Cypern, ihrer physischen und organischen Natur nach, Wien 1885. Illustration p. 59.
Zypern gestern – Gravuren, Nicosia 1983 (reprint). Illustrations pp. 37, 39, 77, 79.

All other photographs are by Gerhard P. Müller.
Gerhard P. Müller uses a Leica R4 camera and Leica lenses from 19 to 250 mm.